Visual Design of GraphQL Data

A Practical Introduction with Legacy Data and Neo4j

Thomas Frisendal

Apress®

Visual Design of GraphQL Data: A Practical Introduction with
Legacy Data and Neo4j

Thomas Frisendal
Copenhagen S, Denmark

ISBN-13 (pbk): 978-1-4842-3903-2   ISBN-13 (electronic): 978-1-4842-3904-9
https://doi.org/10.1007/978-1-4842-3904-9

Library of Congress Control Number: 2018956408

Managing Director, Apress Media LLC: Welmoed Spahr
Acquisitions Editor: Steve Anglin
Development Editor: Matthew Moodie
Coordinating Editor: Mark Powers

Cover designed by eStudioCalamar

Cover image designed by Freepik (www.freepik.com)

Distributed to the book trade worldwide by Springer Science+Business Media New York, 233 Spring Street, 6th Floor, New York, NY 10013. Phone 1-800-SPRINGER, fax (201) 348-4505, e-mail orders-ny@springer-sbm.com, or visit www.springeronline.com. Apress Media, LLC is a California LLC and the sole member (owner) is Springer Science + Business Media Finance Inc (SSBM Finance Inc). SSBM Finance Inc is a **Delaware** corporation.

For information on translations, please e-mail editorial@apress.com; for reprint, paperback, or audio rights, please email bookpermissions@springernature.com.

Apress titles may be purchased in bulk for academic, corporate, or promotional use. eBook versions and licenses are also available for most titles. For more information, reference our Print and eBook Bulk Sales web page at http://www.apress.com/bulk-sales.

Any source code or other supplementary material referenced by the author in this book is available to readers on GitHub via the book's product page, located at www.apress.com/9781484239032. For more detailed information, please visit http://www.apress.com/source-code.

Printed on acid-free paper

*My wonderful wife, Ellen-Margrethe Soelberg,
has again experienced a period of having an author
in the house, yet she has at the same time undertaken
the proof-reading job in her usual, professional manner.
Thank You!.*

Table of Contents

About the Author

Thomas Frisendal is an experienced database consultant with more than 30 years on the IT vendor side and as an independent consultant. He has worked with databases and data modeling since the late 70s; since 1995 primarily on data warehouse projects. He has a strong urge to visualize everything as graphs - even datamodels! He excels in the art of turning data into information and knowledge. His approach to information-driven analysis and design is "New Nordic" in the sense that it represents the traditional Nordic values such as superior quality, functionality, reliability and innovation by new ways of communicating the structure and meaning of the business context.

He lives in Copenhagen, Denmark. His firm, TF Informatik, was founded in 1995 and is registered in Denmark (DK66048950). He is on LinkedIn and Twitter @VizDataModeler[1]. Thomas is an active writer and speaker.

His recent book about Graph Data Modeling[2] has a lot of background and in-depth guidance on most of what has been presented in this book. It proposes property graph modeling as a general modeling paradigm. It has many examples from many contexts.

---

[1]https://twitter.com/VizDataModeler
[2]https://technicspub.com/graph-data-modeling/

Figure 1. *Graph Data Modeling*

About the Technical Reviewer

Ahmed Mohammed is an experienced full stack Java/Angular Developer. He is skilled in Java, JavaScript, CI/CD, Spring Boot, GraphQL, GraphQL Apollo, Linux, Microservices in Cloud, and Angular 2/5. He has an MSc and BSc of Information Technology focused in Web Technologies.

Acknowledgments

Named relationships is one of the fundamental recommendations of this book. The importance of this was made originally by Prof. Joseph D. Novak, who was one of the fathers of Concept Mapping in the development of the psychology of learning.

GraphQL is designed by Facebook, Copyright © 2015-2016. It is now an open source project, where the software is available under a BSD 3 license. Refer to `www.graphQL.org`[1] for more information.

The GraphQL @relation schema directive originated at Graphcool, refer to `www.graph.cool`[2] for more information.

The chapter about using GraphQL with a new graph database draws heavily on a blogpost Five Common GraphQL Problems and How Neo4j-GraphQL Aims To Solve Them[3] written by Will Lyon of Neo4j[4]. I am quoting from it with the author's kind permission. Thank you!

---

[1]`http://www.graphQL.org`
[2]`http://www.graph.cool`
[3]`https://blog.grandstack.io/five-common-graphql-problems-and-how-neo4j-graphql-aims-to-solve-them-e9a8999c8d43`
[4]`https://neo4j.com`

Introduction

You know the basics of GraphQL, but you are still uncertain about how to get business content and API structures right in GraphQL?

GraphQL is indeed an attractive data API for applications (and people).

The GraphQL Schema is pivotal to the success of a GraphQL API. Most development projects involve many stakeholders. There are the developers, of course, and there are business experts as well as application owners, who are to consume the content of the API. This means that the schema is not only a scope contract, but also the authoritative source of structure and meaning of the context covered by the API. There are many other contexts, where complex structures and semantics must be communicated effecetively between a number of people with various backgrounds. And the trick invariably turns out to be: *Use good visualizations!*

The main proposition of this book is graph visualization: GraphQL Schema structure and meaning must be visualized, and the book shows you how. Since the schema is a **"data graph"** containing related concepts in a network organized as a directed graph, the increasingly popular *property graph paradigm* is very appropriate for visualizing GraphQL structures and semantics.

The second theme of this book is that of quality. GraphQL APIs can be used in many constellations possibly including legacy data and/or externally sourced data. Quality must be ensured in all cases. Both on the definitional level (business terminology etc.) and on the data content level (meaningful presentation of the data in business-friendly formats). The book summarizes the top 10 most important focal areas of such quality assurance remedies.

In this edition of the book, the following was added:

- Catching up with the latest version of the GraphQL specifikation (minor adjustments)

- Brief explanation of "schema stitching" etc. and the impact of it on development style

- Discussion of resolver requirements, in particular vis-a-vis legacy SQL data

- Explanation of the Neo4j-GraphQL integration and a look at applying GraphQL to both existing and new Neo4j graph databases.

In this manner, the (data and metadata quality) challenges of front-ending old and new databases with a GraphQL API is the third theme of this book.

The book contains simple guidelines based on lessons learned from real life data discovery and unification. This helps developers and architects to get good quality in the resulting API designs. And the visual techniques helps in producing convincing visual communication about the structure of the API designs.

Spending time on schema quality means that developers work from sharp definitions, which in turn leads to greater productivity and well-structured applications.

CHAPTER 1

Visual Design of GraphQL Data

What Is GraphQL and Why Is Design Important?

GraphQL is getting a lot of interest. GraphQL is a Facebook open source project that has its primary information site at http://graphql.org/.[1]

My interest is the relationship between GraphQL and design. That relationship is certainly very real. In graphql.org's own words:

> "Describe what's possible with a type system. GraphQL APIs are organized in terms of types and fields, not endpoints. Access the full capabilities of your data from a single endpoint. GraphQL uses types to ensure apps only ask for what's possible and provide clear and helpful errors. Apps can use types to avoid writing manual parsing code."

The gist of GraphQL can be seen in the example in Figure 1-1, from graphql.org.

---

[1]http://graphql.org/

© Thomas Frisendal 2018
T. Frisendal, *Visual Design of GraphQL Data*,
https://doi.org/10.1007/978-1-4842-3904-9_1

```
{                               type Query {
  hero {                          hero: Character
    name                        }
    friends {
      name                      type Character {
      homeWorld {                 name: String
        name                      friends: [Character]
        climate                   homeWorld: Planet
      }                           species: Species
      species {                 }
        name
        lifespan                type Planet {
        origin {                  name: String
          name                    climate: String
        }                       }
      }
    }                           type Species {
  }                               name: String
}                                 lifespan: Int
                                  origin: Planet
                                }
```

Figure 1-1. *GraphQL simple example*

The context of Figure 1-1 is *Star Wars* metadata. And what you see to the right is actually part of a GraphQL Schema. What you see on the left could well be a query to the API, and the resulting set of data will share exactly that (data) structure.

The open GraphQL project started in 2012 and belongs in the software architecture universe talked about as APIs these days. In Facebook's own terms: "... GraphQL [is] a query language created by Facebook in 2012 for describing the capabilities and requirements of data models for client-server applications" (GraphQL on GitHub[2]).

---

[2]http://facebook.github.io/graphql/October2016/

The graphql.org site does a nice job of explaining, so I will not repeat all of that here. Graphcool has a nice blog post called "GraphQL Server Basics: The Schema",[3] which includes a good introduction to structure and behavior of GraphQL. William Lyon of Neo4j (http://www.neo4j.com/[4]) has made an excellent overview of GraphQL, which is available as a "refcard" from Dzone at GraphQL Refcard[5] (login is required).

The best tool for getting structure and meaning right is visualization of the graphs. The property graph approach is very powerful for database design across many different data stores. And it is equally well suited for design of data-level APIs, as you will see in this book.

Also notice that the most developers today only have indented bracket displays with "prettify" functionality available. Type completion, driven by the GraphQL Schema, is also available.

Note   There are a few "boxes and arrows" POC-level diagramming tools on the web. See for example GraphQL Voyager,[6] GraphQL Visualizer GraphQL Visualizer,[7] or GraphQL Rover.[8] All of them are "after the fact" in the sense that they visualize from the schema definition. (And they are, to my regret, in the legacy boxes-and-arrows style.)

High-quality data designs are possible only if you get the structure and the meaning right, and that is what this book is about.

---

[3]https://blog.graph.cool/graphql-server-basics-the-schema-ac5e2950214e
[4]http://www.neo4j.com/
[5]https://dzone.com/refcardz/an-overview-of-graphql
[6]https://apis.guru/graphql-voyager/
[7]http://nathanrandal.com/graphql-visualizer/
[8]https://brbb.github.io/graphql-rover/

Issues with Defining Data Structures in GraphQL

As you know, GraphQL is not a database, but it is an API of data, which is described in (and produced from) a set of *GraphQL schema(s).* Since so much relies on the schema, you need to ensure it has high quality.

You are also looking at servers producing data from many different sources, legacy or new. Whatever kind of source, there may be quality issues. *Garbage in equals garbage out.* For that reason, GraphQL API design may take you into having to resolve data discovery and unification issues, such as quality, metadata, and business acceptance.

The focus should always be on the application or business-facing aspects of the interface exposed by the GraphQL server, based on the definitions in the server-side schema.

Consider these guidelines and issues for a GraphQL API:

- Structural mistakes (many-to-many et al.) should be avoided.

- Meaning must be provided and preserved in business terms—in the end, business people will meet the model through the tools.

- Uniqueness must be provided.

- Identity should also be nurtured, just like in a data model.

- The presentation of the data through the API should present ("prettify", if you will) the data in business- and developer-friendly manners—including handling missing or bad data.

- The model should essentially be hierarchical, so care should be spent on nursing the hierarchies and their levels, just like one would do in a multidimensional model.

- In particular, the traversal of many-to-many data structures in the underlying data model should be carefully understood when the API structures that span such relationships are set up.

The major value proposition of this book is to illustrate how issues like these are handled in the GraphQL environment by way of adding visualizations in the property graph style.

Issues with Data Content in GraphQL

Handling the garbage-in/garbage-out dilemma is a matter of:

- Getting to know the data better (a.k.a. data discovery)
- Unifying data from disparate sources (a.k.a. data unification).

There is (too) much information about data preparation and ETL on the Internet and in books (including one of mine). In the GraphQL context, you should be observant of these 10 most important issues:

- Including business names in the API
- Providing identity and uniqueness
- Presenting the keys
- Presenting state changes
- Presenting versions of data
- Presenting dates and times
- Presenting relationships and missing references
- Determining which objects and which relationships
- Presenting the right level of detail
- Developing good relationships

How much work is necessary on the resolver side really depends on these issues, most of which are partly out of your control:

- The quality of the data sources by themselves (structure, meaning, and content)

- Conflicts arising from unification of data from multiple sources (both upstream and down-stream)

We will look at these issues in later chapters of this book. First, we need to deconstruct the GraphQL language.

CHAPTER 2

GraphQL Concepts

There are a number of concepts defined in the GraphQL context. The concept model shown in Figure 2-1 lays out all the important ones.

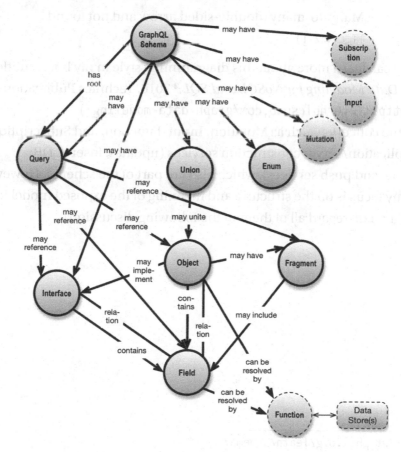

Figure 2-1. *GraphQL concepts*

T. Frisendal, *Visual Design of GraphQL Data*,
https://doi.org/10.1007/978-1-4842-3904-9_2

7

(Refer to the GraphQL Schema introduction at http://graphql.org/ learn/schema/ for all the schema details.[1]) A few words on the diagram style shown in Figure 2-1:

- It is a directed graph (of the concept map category)

- Relationships are named

- Relationships may be:
    - One-to-one (no arrows)

    - One-to-many (arrow)

    - Many-to-many (double-sided arrow and not found Figure 2-1).

You can learn more about this diagramming style in my book entitled *Graph Data Modeling for NoSQL and SQL*,[2] 2016, Technics Publications (visit https://technicspub.com/graph-data-modeling/).

Some concepts, such as Mutation, Input, Function, and Subscription, are application/server construction services (updates, inserts, DB mapping, and push services), which also are part of the schema. However, since my focus is on the structure and meaning of the exposed model in its own right, I disregard all of them in the following discussion.

---

[1]http://graphql.org/learn/schema/
[2]https://technicspub.com/graph-data-modeling/

The rest of the concepts are pretty much what their names imply. Here are some one-liner explanations:

Concept	Explanation
GraphQL Schema	Defines the structure and the meaning of the exposed data model (as well as the data-manipulation functions, which we do not look at here).
Enum	Basically a list of values, which can be applied to a field.
Query	The root query defines the anchor point of the application graph (tree) and shapes the result sets.
Interface	Essentially a "view" of an object (or query); it is frequently used for "subtyping".
Union	A concatenation of results sub-graphs sharing related content. For example various types of persons, as in users, actors, etc.
Object	A business object (think Movie or Starship in the *Star Wars* example).
Fragment	A subset of a sub-graph. Inline fragments are typically used with union-constructs.
Field	The data-bearing things. Can be scalars or lists (yes, like in repeating groups).
Directive	User-definable extensions to the GraphQL syntax.

@relation is a good example of a GraphQL directive. It is introduced by Graphcool[3] (see http://www.graph.cool/). I like it very much, because it names the relationships.

Otherwise you just connect object types like this:

```
Type Movie { ..... actors: [Actor] } )
```

---

[3]http://www.graph.cool

In general, reusable GraphQL schema directives can be used for a variety of purposes:

- Enforcing access permissions

- Formatting date strings

- Auto-generating resolver functions for a particular backend

- Marking strings for internationalization

- Synthesizing globally unique identifiers

- Specifying caching behavior

- Skipping, including, or deprecating fields

- And much more

See the blog post from Ben Newman[4] at https://dev-blog.apollodata.com/reusable-graphql-schema-directives-131fb3a177d1 for all the details.

Note that in the latest working draft of the GraphQL specification[5] (see https://github.com/facebook/graphql/blob/master/spec/GraphQL.md), the following types can be extended by user-defined extensions: Scalars, Objects, Interfaces, Unions, Enums, and InputObjects. This might be used, for example, by a local service to represent data a GraphQL client only accesses locally, or by a GraphQL service that is itself an extension of another GraphQL service. The extensions can be constants, directives, or field definitions.

The syntax graph of the schema parts, which we are interested in, looks like Figure 2-2 on the meta level.

---

[4]https://dev-blog.apollodata.com/reusable-graphql-schema-directives-131fb3a177d1

[5]https://github.com/facebook/graphql/blob/master/spec/GraphQL.md

10

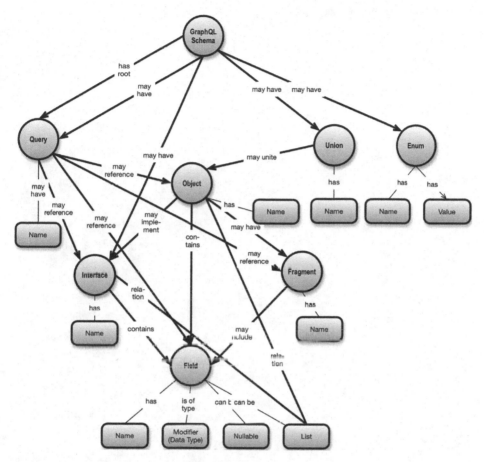

Figure 2-2. *GraphQL syntax elements*

The rounded rectangles signify properties of the concepts (object types) they are connected to.

Let's look at data design issues in general and determine which of those are relevant in the GraphQL API context.

CHAPTER 3

Getting Started

Which Design Levels?

Classical data modeling failed in a number of ways. We have to do better than that. What did not work well was conceptual modeling, which has faded away in favor of what one could call "The Great Pragmatic and Quick, Unified Data Modeling Practice".

Today many development organizations have a one-step approach to modeling, which is performed when necessary in the development process. Logical and physical models have come together. The driving force is time to delivery, and what the unified process is trying to answer are two aspects of developing a good solution:

- Describing the "what" in terms of a logical data model

- Describing some aspects of the "how," e.g., physical access optimization for better performance

In the GraphQL context, the aim is complete independence between applications (or users) and data stores. Since we (in this book) are only interested in the schema(s) and queries, we should focus on the "what" question.

© Thomas Frisendal 2018
T. Frisendal, *Visual Design of GraphQL Data*,
https://doi.org/10.1007/978-1-4842-3904-9_3

In other words, we need a fresh take on the conceptual level. It still adds business value, because it is a tool to communicate effectively with business folks about things like terminology, relationships, and the like. This is why visualization techniques must play a dominant role.

Secondly, we should also nurse the "logical level," since it (the schema) is a designed artifact encompassing design decisions about scope, generalizations, abstractions and aggregations, relationships and presentation. Again, visualization is a great tool for understanding and for communication.

For the physical level we have various use cases of the resolver functions. We look at some of the requirements in chapters toward the end of the book. We describe some considerations, which can influence the resolver functionality, but we are not giving specific code examples, such as JavaScript or similar.

But let us start at the top. A good way to get going is to try to understand and scope the subject area.

Getting an Overview

If you don't know the scope already, you need to get an overview of a subject area that you are creating a schema for.

Figure 3-1 shows an overview of some business concepts in a car dealership.

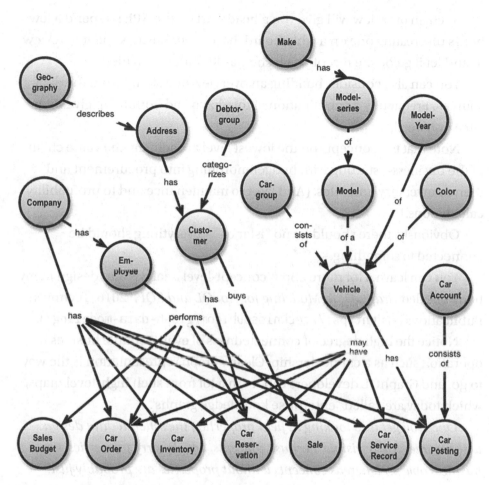

Figure 3-1. *Car dealership concepts overview*

Notice how the upper levels tend to be classifications and other hierarchies. The levels in the middle are the core business objects engaged in the business processes.

The concepts at the lowest level are, interestingly enough, all business events or other records, some of which are the snapshot type (like inventory on a given date).

15

Such an overview will give you a head start on the API, so spend a few hours on creating one on a whiteboard, have other business people review it, and let it guide the rest of your schema-definition activities.

You can also consider building an overview bottom up from the data sources. Frequently a combination of top down and bottom up gives you what you need.

Note that the concepts on the lowest level are actually the value chain of the business—starting with budget morphing into procurement and then to inventory and sales. (And later to maintenance and to profitability calculations.)

Obviously, there should be no "islands"—everything should be connected to something.

You can learn a lot more about concept-level analysis and design in my book entitled *Graph Data Modeling for NoSQL and SQL*,[1] 2016, Technics Publications (visit `https://technicspub.com/graph-data-modeling/`).

Notice the high degree of connectedness of even a simple business operation such as a car dealership. Clearly graph representation is the way to go, and GraphQL developers can learn a lot from such high-level maps, which today are called "enterprise knowledge graphs".

Once you get into looking at field properties, the schema data design will become clearly visible, because concepts, which carry properties, are business objects, whereas concepts without properties are probably just abstractions, which you may wish to get rid of, or describe with properties, as appropriate.

Note that even though you should try to map the enterprise (on a high-level concept map), you should not take too many, or too big, steps. In fact, recent developments in the GraphQL community encourage a stepwise approach and reuse of existing schema parts together with freshly developed schema parts. We will return briefly to this (schema stitching and schema binding) in a later chapter.

---

[1] `https://technicspub.com/graph-data-modeling/`

We are looking at defining GraphQL schemas and APIs. The physical gofers are hidden in resolver functions and we will mention them in the last part of this book.

Our focus is on both the business aspects of meaning of content and also on the structural aspects of related data.

To be precise, what we are looking for is:

- Meaning

- Structure

This is why graph visualization is the universal key to looking at structured information.

It is fair to say that the visual parts of this book propose the property graph modeling style as the best design pattern for GraphQL schemas.

CHAPTER 4

An Email Example

The GraphQL Schema is a *data graph* containing related concepts in a network, organized as a directed graph. In a way, you could say that the GraphQL approach makes everything look like a graph! (Which is actually the case, anyway.)

This makes the so-called property graph approach to graph visualization a powerful opportunity for the GraphQL Schema designer.

We will work from a simple email graph data model. First let's get an overview of the basic concepts of email (as defined in the Internet Message Format standard called RFC 5322). See Figure 4-1.

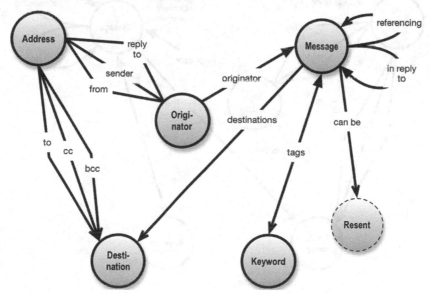

Figure 4-1. *Email concepts overview*

© Thomas Frisendal 2018
T. Frisendal, *Visual Design of GraphQL Data*,
https://doi.org/10.1007/978-1-4842-3904-9_4

Figure 4-1 is loyal to the terminology actually used in the Internet standard. This gives rise to issues, if you try to build a classic, normalized data model from this, which we discuss shortly.

Notice that some relationships are one-to-one (for example, Originator from Address), whereas other are many-to-many (e.g., Keyword tags Message). There are also some one-to-many relationships. We will come back to this issue, but please make a mental note of this:

**Caveat: Relationship cardinalities matter, because although GraphQL is a directed graph paradigm, the set of possible queries within a GraphQL Schema is a subset of sub-graphs all originating as sub-trees from the root query. **

Descoping a little bit: This email subject area is a bit complex, so let's skip the business of resending messages for now.

Let's move on to describe the scope of the GraphQL data scope in the form of a detailed property graph, as shown in Figure 4-2.

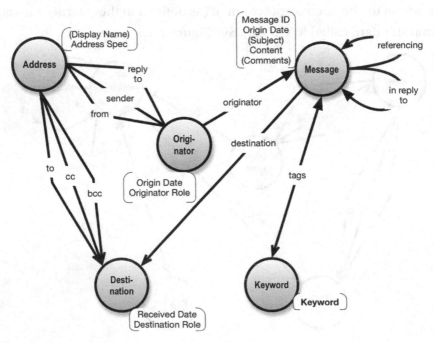

Figure 4-2. *Email as a property graph*

Notice that Figure 4-2 adds little property boxes to the concept model. This is a compact way of describing structure and content in the same diagram. This makes the diagram a true property graph model. (You can learn much more about property graphs in my *book entitled Graph Data Modeling for NoSQL and SQL*,[1] 2016, Technics Publications. See `https://technicspub.com/graph-data-modeling/`.)

To recap, the circles are *concepts*, which are the *nodes* of the graph. A message, for example, is a concept, and it is part of several relationships, such as the originator (who sent the message) or "in reply to" (which other message is replying to). The properties can be attached to concepts (nodes) and/or relationships (edges of the graph).

The notation uses arrowheads for cardinalities. In Figure 4-2, you find one-to-one, one-to-many, and many-to-many relationships. For a brief explanation of property graphs,[2] see `http://bit.ly/2hMNYvE`.

In the GraphQL context, the property graph is useful for representing the structure of the schema:

- *Nodes are types (object types, interface types, and union types)*

- *Relationships represent the connections between types*

- *Properties are the fields of the types (scalars or lists)*

Note   As a matter of fact, if you are willing to "forget" some of the business concepts (like "Originator" and "Destination," you can reduce the model to be more compact. See Figure 4-3.

---

[1] `https://technicspub.com/graph-data-modeling/`
[2] `http://bit.ly/2hMNYvE`

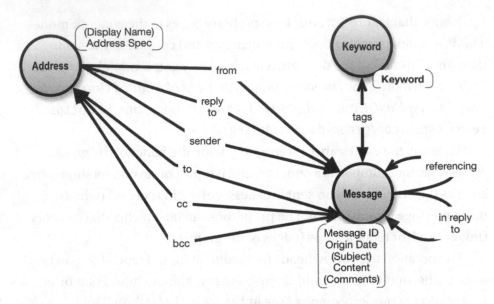

Figure 4-3. *Email property graph simplified*

Notice that in the compact version shown in Figure 4-3, there are more M:M relationships. A logical model like that (yes, logical models may include M:M) is problematic with SQL source, but makes good sense in a graph database.

Note that in property graphs, the relationships are named. This is important because those names are part of the business semantics, and by visualizing them, it is much easier to review and discuss the meaning imposed by the structure. Graphcool offers a @relation directive for getting the names of the relationships into the schema. This is a very good idea.

The property graph representation is considerably more compact than the "boxes and arrows" method found in most diagramming approaches. In the GraphQL space, there is a tool called GraphQL Voyager[3] (https://apis.guru/graphql-voyager/). The Voyager is based

---

[3]https://apis.guru/graphql-voyager/

on a standard data model diagramming library, which is in the "boxes and arrows" style. Getting a solid grip on the structure across, say, five or eight object types is not easy. The property graph representation is much more compact and has been successful over the last 15 years, and it comes out of the Nordics. Neo4J,[4] based in Malmö, invented the property graph model as a data model, and they are now a leading player in the graph database segment worldwide. The property graph style proposed here was designed by the author in his 2016 book on *Graph Data Modeling for SQL and NoSQL.*[5]

At this point, we have dealt with schema visualization, and that makes GraphQL pretty and good:

- Alignment with business terminology and definitions (structure and content fields)

- Understanding complex schemas, structured as graphs

Expressed in the GraphQL Schema Definition Language (SDL), the (non-compacted) email data model could be specified along these lines:

```
1    #
2    # Email Graph Data Model
3    #
4    # GraphQL Schema
5    #
6    # Based on Internet Message Format RFC5322, but simplified
        somewhat
7    #
8    # Copyright Thomas Frisendal, 2017
9    #
10
```

---

[4]https://neo4j.com/
[5]https://technicspub.com/graph-data-modeling/

```
11    scalar Datetime
12    scalar AddrSpec
13    enum destination_role {
14      To
15      Cc
16      Bcc
17    }
18
19    enum originator_role {
20      From
21      Sender
22      Reply to
23    }
24
25    type Address {
26      id: ID!
27      display_name: String
28      address_spec: AddrSpec!
29      address_from: Originator! @relation(name: "From")
30      address_sender: Originator @relation(name: "Sender")
31      address_reply_to: Originator @relation(name: "ReplyTo")
32      destination_to: [Destination] @relation(name: "To")
33      destination_cc: [Destination] @relation(name: "Cc")
34      destination_bcc: [Destination] @relation(name: "Bcc")
35    }
36
37    type Originator {
38      id: ID!
39      origin_date: Datetime!
40      originator_role: originator_role!
41      message: [Message!] @relation(name: "Originator")
42      address_from: Address! @relation(name: "From")
```

```
43      address_sender: Address @relation(name: "Sender")
44      address_reply_to: Address @relation(name: "ReplyTo")
45    }
46
47    type Destination {
48      id: ID!
49      destination_role: destination_role!
50      received_date: Datetime!
51      message: Message! @relation(name: "Destination")
52      address_to: [Address]! @relation(name: "To")
53      address_cc: [Address] @relation(name: "Cc")
54      address_bcc: [Address] @relation(name: "Bcc")
55    }
56
57    type Message {
58      id: ID!
59      subject: String
60      comments: String
61      originator: Originator! @relation(name: "Originator")
62      destinations: [Destination]! @relation(name:
        "HasDestination")
63      referencing: [Message] @relation(name: "Referencing")
64      in_reply_to: [Message] @relation(name: "InReplyTo")
65      keywords: [Keyword] @relation(name: "Tags")
66    }
67
68    type Keyword {
69      id: ID!
70      keyword: String! @isUnique
71      messages: [Message] @relation(name: "Tags")
72    }
73
```

```
74    type Query {
75      messages(limit: Int = 20): [Message]!
76    }
77
78    schema {
79      query: Query
80    }
```

Note that this example uses the Graphcool-invented schema directive @relation, which, not the least, names the relationships. This is a feature that I strongly recommend.

Also note that the schema code is not complete and will probably give syntax errors if you try to use it directly. GraphQL platforms do have extensions of their own. This example, when used on Graphcool, has issues with underscores and missing @model directives, for example. On the other hand, a subset of this example was used with Neo4j as a basis for a new graph database, without problems.

Also note that the property graph diagram is many times easier to read and understand than the schema definition syntax!

Let's see what kinds of issues this design could contain.

CHAPTER 5

Business Meaning

The meaning part is really owned by the business. The business folks have the privilege of deciding on their terminology. Applications or microservices are business facing and should talk the language of the business. That goes for the data content as well.

Data Names in the API Matter

Since many physical data stores may be schema free or schema-on-read, where the "schema" is inferred when reading the data, we need a layer of presentation to business users, using business terms. That layer is our GraphQL API.

Even more challenging is that much of the (big) data that people want to analyze is more or less machine generated or system generated. Again, this calls for a user-facing data terminology layer toward the business environment. Finally, even in integration projects, standardizing business names is necessary to obtain acceptance in the business user community.

Names include object type names (e.g., originator), property names (e.g., display name of the address), and relationship names (e.g., cc).

Relationship names are important because they are also used to infer the type of the relationship (dependency). Action verbs indicate activity on business objects, whereas weak verbs like "has" etc. indicate ordinary functional dependencies between an identifier of a business object type and its properties.

© Thomas Frisendal 2018
T. Frisendal, *Visual Design of GraphQL Data*,
https://doi.org/10.1007/978-1-4842-3904-9_5

Relationships are bidirectional, as shown in Figure 5-1.

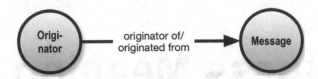

Figure 5-1. *Read from right to left or vice versa*

For those reasons, names matter. However, I tend only to write the name coming from the parent. That is the "originator" in this case, since left-to-right ordering is applied (Western cultural conventions).

What is important is that some linking phrases (the names of relationships) contain verbs, and verbs imply that an "actor" makes something happen. In other words, the relationship denotes something, which is more than a plain property depending on the identity of something. This makes the target a candidate for being identified as a business object type.

Names should be backed up by solid definitions (as comments or descriptions) wherever there is risk of ambiguity. Definitions of core business concepts last a long time and reach many people. This means that they should not only be precise and to the point, they should also communicate well and be easy to remember.

Names should be as specific as they can get. For example, avoid using Address if what you are talking about is Destination Address.

Note that GraphQL has a nice, simple way to support subtyping by way of defined interfaces. In the email example, we could consider setting up Originator and Destination as interfaces, both implementing a Contact type. It would look like the following.

First as the two types:

```
1    type Originator {
2        id: ID!
3        origin_date: Datetime!
```

```
4      message: : [Message!]  @relation(name: "Originator")
5      address_from: Address! @relation(name: "From")
6      address_sender: Address @relation(name: "Sender")
7      address_reply_to: Address @relation(name: "ReplyTo")
8   }
9
10   type Destination {
11      id: ID!
12      destination_role: destination_role!
13      received_date: Datetime!
14      message: Message! @relation(name: "Destination")
15      address_to: [Address]! @relation(name: "To")
16      address_cc: [Address] @relation(name: "Cc")
17      address_bcc: [Address] @relation(name: "Bcc")
18   }
```

And here is an interface construct:

```
1   interface Contact {
2      id: ID!
3   }
4
5   type Originator implements Contact {
6   origin_date: Datetime!
7     message: [Message!] @relation(name: "Originator")
8     address_from: Address! @relation(name: "From")
9     address_sender: Address @relation(name: "Sender")
10    address_reply_to: Address @relation(name: "ReplyTo")
11   }
12
13   type Destination implements Contact {
14   destination_role: destination_role!
15     received_date: Datetime!
```

```
16      message: Message! @relation(name: "Destination")
17      address_to: [Address]! @relation(name: "To")
18      address_cc: [Address] @relation(name: "Cc")
19      address_bcc: [Address] @relation(name: "Bcc")
20    }
```

We did not use interfaces in our email design, because the overlap between the two are minimal. However, interface names should also be valid business names.

The quality of the content of the API results depends on the business semantics and on the actual data delivered by the API. We dealt with the structure and the terminology in the property graphs, so next we need to handle the actual data content properly. However, remember that meaning and content go together. If you change the semantics, then you may have to refactor the data.

Note   Do name checks of the content of the property graph(s) together with some subject area experts to get the semantics sorted out.

In cases of mismatch between business terminology and the data names in the databases, somebody will have to do something at the resolver level. More about that later.

Finding Standard Data Structures

Another thing to think about before you set up the schema is standard patterns. Many areas of various kinds of business activities and ditto objects have already been defined as best practice data models.

For example, a `Company Location` property seems to be a bit under-designed. Locations are geographical addresses, which are business addresses. There are several best practices out there for many general object types. See for example `schema.org` or various national or international standards.

How can we detect that something is missing about, for example, company locations? One indicator could be that the precise linking phrase contains an action verb: `located at`. Action verbs tend to denote relationships between object types, not between objects and their properties.

So, looking for standard patterns is another check to do before releasing your schema.

Establishing Identity and Uniqueness

The days of analyzing functional dependencies, looking for candidate keys, and so on, are now behind us. But we still need to deal with identity and uniqueness. Since the GraphQL schema is a directed graph, identity and uniqueness of nodes must happen at the schema level.

What is the issue? The trouble is that we—as humans—do not really care a lot about uniqueness. What is in a name, anyway? We all know that James Brown can refer to a large number of individuals. The trick that we use, is to add context like "Yes, you know, James Brown, the singer, the godfather of soul". So, when it really matters, context is the definite answer. But if a node represents a person called James Brown, we will look at the context to try to infer who we are talking about.

Fortunately, we are in a connected graph (the schema), which means that we should look at the immediate vicinity and infer identity and uniqueness from there.

Identity is functionally derived from uniqueness, which sets the context.

Another way of putting it is that identity is really the scope of what the properties apply to (see Figure 5-2).

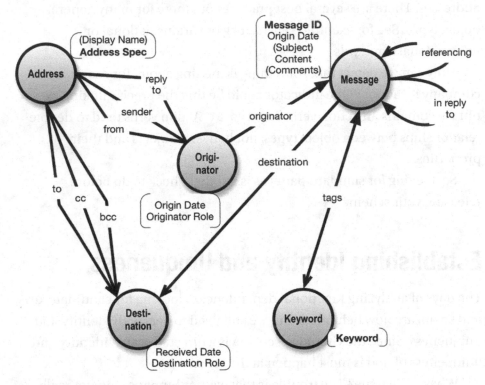

Figure 5-2. *Identity is driven by uniqueness*

Received Date shares scope with Destination Role and both are driven by the identity of Destination. For now, it suffices to say that we need to establish a reliable identity of Destination. (This used to be called "finding the primary key".)

Uniqueness is the matter of identifying what, on the business level, makes an identity unique.

Yes, the Destination is uniquely defined by the combination of Message and Address (whatever their identities are defined as). Enforcing uniqueness is also an important task in the design of an API schema. (Previously this was the realm of "foreign keys".)

There are no good reasons for adding visual icons or special markers, because the uniqueness is implied by the structure. But I did highlight in bold Address Spec, Message ID, and Keyword (the property) since they are, by a business definition, unique.

In conclusion, identity determines the scope of a property (e.g., Received Date applies to Destination) and uniqueness determines the business-level criteria for ensuring uniqueness in the interface (e.g., Destinations must be unique across the combination of the identities of Address and Message). Note that so far we are talking business level. In most cases, these issues are likely to have been solved by way of IT-generated "surrogate keys" in the databases.

At least in northern Europe (where I am from), using assigned identification numbers such as social security numbers is not generally advisable. They are not guaranteed to stay unique and to persist. Inventing new "natural identities" can be very practical for us in IT, right? We have been the ones driving that trend over the years. Business people do not object too much, and at times they can see why such keys are practical.

Here are some rules for finding uniqueness and identities in the diagrams:

- The uniqueness of an object is determined by the relationships coming to it from the concepts that are higher up.

- The identity of an object is thus the combined identities of the referencing concepts.

- Properties, on the other hand, share the identity of the object that they are depending on, which is the defining criteria of a property.

So, using these simple, visual inspection methods, we can conclude the context and hence the uniqueness of each object type, at the business level:

Object Type	Uniqueness
Address	Address Spec
Originator	Address Spec, Message ID, originator_role
Destination	Address Spec, Message ID, destination_role
Message	Message ID
Keyword	Keyword ID, Message ID

Let's recap the identity and uniqueness issues:

Uniqueness is the business-level rules to determine the uniqueness of the instance of data. Frequently, this is a combination of business-level "keys" such as ticket number, line number, employee number, postal code, product number, and so forth. Identity is the combined result of the uniqueness of participating types. An order line, for example, is unique for the combination of order number (from the Order type) and order line number (from the Order Line type). In most IT systems, identity is ensured by way of a unique ID field (the primary key in relational databases) or other kinds of surrogate keys. Obviously, ID conflicts across multiple source databases must be resolved. Also note that the downstream requirements of the GraphQL API data may set distinct requirements of the API's delivery of identity and uniqueness.

Mismatches may be fixed at the resolver layer. More about that later on when we look at connecting the database to the API.

Establishing the business meaning and its rules is obviously important. Equally important is to design good ways to facilitate navigation of the business flow, which is what we look at next.

CHAPTER 6

Presenting the Business Flow

Presenting the Keys

In order for applications and business users to get easy access to the network of objects and events that mirror the business flow, we need to think in terms of navigation of the network. This starts with the issue of making identification easy.

Clearly the many concatenated identity components on the business side (uniqueness rules) are not practical. As API designers, we are allowed to invent things. One category of creatable things is known as "keys".

Working with large concatenated keys, for example, is really not very practical. We much prefer the preciseness of unique, simple (one variable) fields. This was first established in 1976 (in an early object oriented context). It soon came to rule the world of primary and foreign keys under the name "surrogate key". It turns out that business-level keys seldom are single-level fields, unless developers building IT solutions define them. Think account numbers, item numbers, postal codes, and the like. And even if reasonably precisely defined concepts were used, they were not always guaranteed to stay unique over a longer period of time. Item numbers, for instance, could be reused over time.

© Thomas Frisendal 2018
T. Frisendal, *Visual Design of GraphQL Data*,
https://doi.org/10.1007/978-1-4842-3904-9_6

Note   There are some important scope considerations in the discussion of keys and IDs.

Many database designs include system-generated keys of the surrogate key kind. These can most likely be reused as "Xxxxxx ID" identity fields in your API design, which is good. The scope of such keys are at the database-instance level, but the surrogate keys may well have been carried over into data warehouse tables and the like.

GraphQL supports "ID" as a scalar type. The scope of such an ID field is within that object type within that application (server), and the ID is mainly for getting data out of the cache. They are unique within that scope, but not more than that.

How will a solution-level data design of email enhanced with system-assigned keys look?

Figure 6-1 is a solution-level property graph and it includes an identifier (Xxxxxxx**Id) in italics for each object type. The purpose of the identifier is to serve as a simple, persistent, unique identifier of the instances of the object. (That is the nature of a surrogate key.) Note that "Message ID" was already in the system (by definition, in the Internet Message Format standard).

If there is no surrogate key scheme in place, and if the data scope needs to be larger than the application, such as for data-level integration purposes downstream, then you are looking at a data architecture design issue.

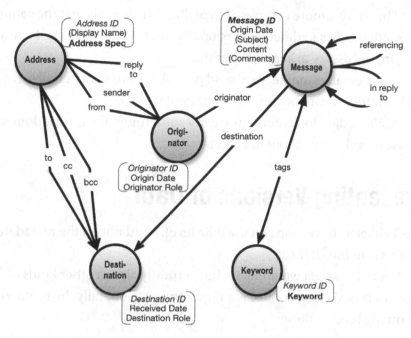

Figure 6-1. *Identities added as key fields (ID)*

Keys can be dealt with at the resolver level. More about that later.

Presenting State Changes

Sometimes you have to handle state changes in the interface. Here we are talking about business state changes. In the financial world, for example, buy/sell transactions in securities are being raised up through a hierarchy that looks something like this:

- Considered

- Planned

- Agreed (done deal)

- Preliminarily booked

- Settled

- Finally accounted for

(This is a bit more complex in real life.) The issue is that the same transaction exists in different versions throughout its lifecycle. Date and time are necessary to keep track of that.

In our email example, we would probably have to materialize (in the API) whether the message was resent (and when).

"Making data look pretty" is clearly something that can be done at the resolver level. More about that later.

Presenting Versions of Data

This brings us to versions on the data level. (And not on the metadata level, such as schema changes.)

Not only in data warehouses, but certainly also in other kinds of applications, version control is a requirement. Generally the requirements are on the level of these:

- Which version is the current one?

- What is the starting point and ending point of a given version (with date and or time precision)?

- When did this version come into existence?

Sometimes backdated corrections are necessary. It could be, for example, correcting a price, which was found to be wrong, at a later point in time.

Keeping two versions depends on accounting practices and possibly also legislative requirements. Be sure to understand what the situation is in your context.

If you are into versioning, you should consider chains of events. (The *next* event following this version of this transaction is XXXXX on date YYYYMMDD, for example.) Graphs are excellent for modeling and implementing that. You might also be interested in prior event chains. (The event that *preceded* this version of this transaction is XXXXX on date YYYYMMDD, for example.) See the discussion about resolving this in a later chapter.

CHAPTER 7

Content Matters

Housekeeping Proper

A recommended best practice is to keep order in your housekeeping—the accountant way, of course. Keep track of who did what and when.

It is a good idea to keep track of things like the following for all object types:

- Who created this record?

- When was the record created?

- Who changed this record the last time?

- When was the date and time of the last change?

- How was this record loaded?

- When was the record loaded?

- What was the source system of the record?

- What are the versioning control dates (from and to)?

- And more...

If such metadata is available in the data sources, I am sure that there are many people out there who would benefit greatly from having them available in the API. Some of this information may be added at the resolver level.

© Thomas Frisendal 2018
T. Frisendal, *Visual Design of GraphQL Data*,
https://doi.org/10.1007/978-1-4842-3904-9_7

Scalar Data Types

When should we worry about data types?

If you have not done so already, now is the time to think about the *API-level* data types. The GraphQL simple scalar types are given beforehand. Just prepare yourself for surprises. You want to consider precision and representation of large numbers needing high precision. With regard to dates and timestamps, you have to define your own custom types. If there are advanced business needs, you need to know this. Refer to the following section on handling time.

The physical data types are not likely going to be the same, but hopefully they are compatible (and mappable in resolver functions). The same goes for type conversions.

Presenting Dates and Times

Date and time are some of the tough challenges in databases, and indeed also in GraphQL. GraphQL is a relatively new framework and it is evolving. At the time of writing, Date can be implemented as a custom scalar type (DIY). There are a number of GitHub projects developing good stuff in this area. See for example GraphQL ISO Date[1] at `https://github.com/ excitement-engineer/graphql-iso-date`.

Dates and times obey some slightly irregular international rules set for the management of time zones, as you know. They are not systematic in the sense that they can be easily derived from the value of the field.

Time zones are indeed difficult to handle. Calendars are somewhat easier, but still subject to a lot of national and cultural variations. If you take a plain vanilla U.S. calendar from the month of February, you will notice that there are two special days that do not apply outside of the United States. Valentine's Day is slowly finding its way into Europe, but there is no Presidents' Day.

---

[1]`https://github.com/excitement-engineer/graphql-iso-date`

If your data model is required to support global operations, you might need at least four variables on everything:

- Local date (pure)

- Local time (no date involved)

- Global date (pure)

- Global time (set to GMT, for example)

See more details about resolving date and time in the resolver chapters.

Using Custom Schema Directives

Date formatting is a good use case for custom schema directives. Ben Newman has a good blog post entitled "Reusable GraphQL Schema Directives[2]," (https://dev-blog.apollodata.com/reusable-graphql-schema-directives-131fb3a177d1), which goes into quite some detail about how to implement those.

Here I will just give you a feel for what it looks like (in Ben Newman's blog post).

First, define a directive with a default format and an argument:

```
1   directive @formattableDate(
2     defaultFormat: String = "mmmm d, yyyy"
3   ) on FIELD_DEFINITION
4
5   scalar Date
6
7   type Query {
8     today: Date @formattableDate
9   }
```

---

[2]https://dev-blog.apollodata.com/reusable-graphql-schema-directives-131fb3a177d1

The directive can be incorporated into a schema and used with different formats:

```
1   import { graphql } from "graphql";
2   import { makeExecutableSchema } from "graphql-tools";
3
4...const schema = makeExecutableSchema({
5     typeDefs,
6     schemaDirectives: {
7       formattableDate: FormattableDateDirective
8     }
9   });
10
11  graphql(schema, `query { today }`).then(result => {
12    // Logs with the default "mmmm d, yyyy" format:
13    console.log(result.data.today);
14  });
15
16  graphql(schema, `query {
17    today(format: "d mmm yyyy")
18  }`).then(result => {
19    // Logs with the requested "d mmm yyyy" format:
20    console.log(result.data.today);
21  });
```

As said, Ben Newman's blog post has all the details that you need to implement this.

Design Is Decisions

Never forget that API schema modeling is about *design*! Design means making decisions that impact the *business quality* of the solution. Obviously there is a dilemma between:

- Supporting the business processes at hand/the business questions in demand (now and in the future)

- Keeping it simple

Strive for a balanced solution between scope and simplicity. Visualizing the design decisions will make your world more simple.

Since we design for the business, in the end, the decisions are up to the business!

Let's move on to the structural matters.

CHAPTER 8

Getting the Structure Right

Which Objects and Which Relationships?

The structure of the data model is, of course, built on the object types and the relationships, which we have already discussed.

But more general issues arise from picking the right objects.

We do have some generally applicable tools in our tool belt, as follows:

- Abstraction, generalization, and specialization (aka aggregation)

- Classification and typing

- Lifecycle dependencies and versioning

- Recognizing hierarchies

There are also some problem areas to be aware of:

- One-to-one relationships

- Many-to-many relationships and nested object types

- Trees (hierarchies of different kinds)

© Thomas Frisendal 2018
T. Frisendal, *Visual Design of GraphQL Data*,
https://doi.org/10.1007/978-1-4842-3904-9_8

One of your best helpers is a good concept model with meaningful linking phrases (names of the dependencies). Creating the model on a whiteboard is often enough. Remember that concepts relate to other concepts in a sentence-like (subject/predicate/object) manner, such as `Customer-places-Order`.

The verbs in those little sentences tell you a lot about the structure. Is the target just a property or not? The inclusion of "is" or "has" indicate a property. Or is it a full-blown relationship between business objects? "Places" indicates a full-blown relationship, because it implies a process that transforms one state of the business to another state.

GraphQL Schema Stitching, Making a Patchwork

GraphQL is moving toward becoming a patchwork of federated servers working together. The new capabilities are called:

- Schema stitching

- Schema delegation

- Schema binding

The discussion quickly becomes technical. Instead, let's focus on the overall consequences.

Basically those new features allow you to:

- Make distributed queries, which get consolidated results from a set of GraphQL schemas/servers.

- Make integrations between your own schema and somebody else's schemas, either at the schema level or at the level of resolvers.

GraphQL has a high level of "self consciousness" thanks to its introspection functionality, and it is strongly typed. This means that the integrations can benefit from having remote servers introspecting one another to determine who can answer what within a query. This also opens up the possibility for publicly available GraphQL APIs (and there are already some of those). So, GraphQL aspires to take the lead in the open data space, which has been dominated by the W3C stack and SPARQL endpoints.

Sashko Stubailo has a nice blog post[1] at `https://dev-blog.apollodata.com/graphql-schema-stitching-8af23354ac37` and a GitHub repository for the most simple level, schema stitching,[2] as shown in Figure 8-1.

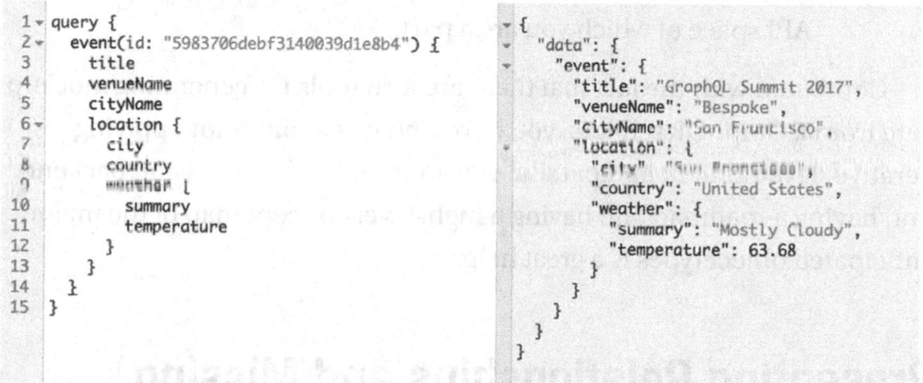

```
 1 ▾ query {
 2 ▾   event(id: "5983706debf3140039d1e8b4") {
 3       title
 4       venueName
 5       cityName
 6 ▾     location {
 7         city
 8         country
 9         weather {
10           summary
11           temperature
12         }
13       }
14     }
15 }
```

```
{
  "data": {
    "event": {
      "title": "GraphQL Summit 2017",
      "venueName": "Bespoke",
      "cityName": "San Francisco",
      "location": {
        "city": "San Francisco",
        "country": "United States",
        "weather": {
          "summary": "Mostly Cloudy",
          "temperature": 63.68
        }
      }
    }
  }
}
```

Figure 8-1. *Schema stitching demo from Stubailo*

What happens in this patchwork is that two queries are being stitched together:

- The event

- The weather forecast

---

[1] https://dev-blog.apollodata.com/graphql-schema-stitching-8af23354ac37
[2] https://github.com/stubailo/schema-stitching-demo

They are in two separate servers, but they know each other's URLs. That way they can do the integration.

See the Apollo documentation[3] (`https://www.apollographql.com/docs/graphql-tools/schema-stitching.html`) for more details.

The consequences are clear:

- You should investigate whether someone else already created (parts of) an API, which you can take advantage of.

- You should not try to solve everything at the same time. Instead, take a patchworking approach.

- You should cooperate and share within your working scope so that everybody contributes to the GraphQL API space of which you are a part.

Combined with the fact that there are also tools for generating mockup data from a GraphQL schema, you have rich possibilities for applying iterative development and parallel development of frontend and backend. But, having a roadmap and having a high-level concept map of the major anticipated object types is a great help.

Presenting Relationships and Missing References

You need to know whether the type of a relationship is that of:

- One-to-one or zero/one to zero/one

- Zero/one to zero/many

- Zero/many to zero/many

---

[3]`https://www.apollographql.com/docs/graphql-tools/schema-stitching.html`

The first alternative can be visualized as connections without arrowheads, as shown in Figure 8-2.

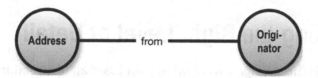

Figure 8-2. *One/zero to one*

The second alternative can be visualized as connections with an arrowhead in the "many" end, as shown in Figure 8-3.

Figure 8-3. *One/zero to zero/many*

The third type of relationship (many-to-many) can be visualized as a connection with arrowheads in both ends, as shown in Figure 8-4.

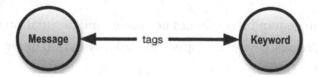

Figure 8-4. *Many to many*

I do not recommend visualizing the starting or ending point as being capable of being "empty," simply because this functionality varies across data stores. Nevertheless, missing references do occur. Look at tags, for example. Some messages are not tagged and some keywords are not used to tag anything.

Resolving missing information, such as outer join situations, must be handled at the resolver level.

Presenting the Right Level of Detail

Abstraction is the strongest weapon in your arsenal. Abstraction works like layers, as shown in Figure 8-5.

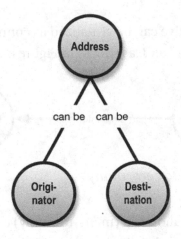

Figure 8-5. *Generalization versus specialization*

So you can generalize originator addresses and destination addresses to be just addresses. Or you can specialize addresses into being originators and destinations.

Note   Moving up a to a higher level layer is generalization; specialization is working your way down into more and more detail.

Generalization make things more broadly useful while at the same time losing some details.

Specialization, on the other hand, gets you more detail, and—consequently—more complexity. Ask your business experts what they really want and need. (Normally they want a bit more than they need, because they fear that this is the only chance of getting it.)

In fact, the compacted version of the email property graph was a generalization, as shown in Figure 8-6.

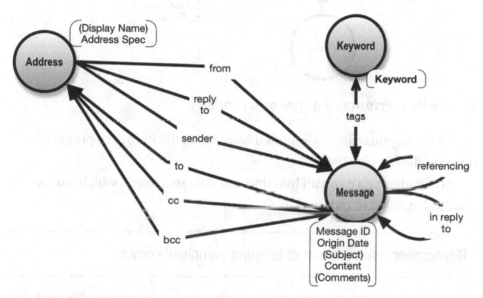

Figure 8-6. *Generalization for simplification*

We have generalized Originator and Destination out of explicit existence. However, the roles they play—"from" "to" and so on—are maintained as relationships in the schema.

Another useful way to reduce referential complexity is to use classification, which is related to specialization. We could have had a concept of "message type" to indicate whether a message is high priority, as shown in Figure 8-7.

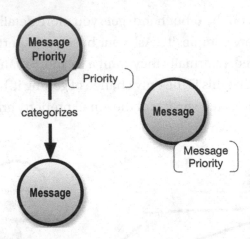

Figure 8-7. *Priority as a type or a property*

Obviously this can be simplified by pushing the `Priority` property down to the `Message` level.

Sometimes you may run into unusual data structures, which can be handled in different manners.

Remember   Always aim at keeping complexity down.

One of the problems with the normalization approach in relational data modeling is that it leads to a plentitude of tables. Some of the tables only serve as placeholders for relationships.

One such scenario is multiple type relationships, which, at times, seem to be logical.

Let us have a look at a 3-way relationship.

Addresses can be used as destinations and destinations can be described as of three roles: to, cc, and bcc. Basically this is a ternary relationship with three participating concepts.

In fact, there is almost always a real business object behind a many-to-many relationship. In multidimensional (data warehouse) modeling, there is a construct called the "factless fact," meaning a fact table without any information other than the foreign keys to the dimensions. Such a table is the mother of all relationships, and in fact (pun intended), even factless facts most often have properties (measures), once you start looking for them. See Figure 8-8.

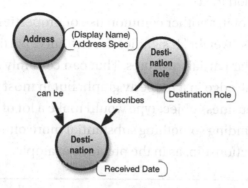

Figure 8-8. *Resolving a 3-way relationship using a "bridge object type"*

Another good way to visualize this ternary relationship is using the property graph models' capability of having properties on relationships.

This works well if your final destination is a property graph database such as Neo4J[4] or the like. See Figure 8-9.

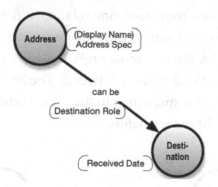

Figure 8-9. *Role as a property of the relationship*

---

[4]http://www.neo4j.com

However, if your data store is a SQL database, you will most likely have the three business object types implemented as three tables. In my opinion the representation of three object types is fair and to the point. Roles do exist and using such classifications on "bridge tables" in a many-to-many relationship is a good idea.

Come to think of it, another common use of properties on the relationship level is "weight". It signifies, for instance, participation or part-ownership or similar partial measures. That can certainly be implemented as a property on the edge in a property graph, but in most peoples' minds, a "participation" business object type would make a lot of sense. This brings us back to finding something substantial more often than not in a many-to-many relationship, as in the previous example.

Note   In GraphQL schemas, relationships—either simple name-name references or the Graphcool schema directive @relation—are non-information bearing. This leaves you with the option of using a specialized object type to carry the properties, which describe the relationship. This is a resolver issue.

Another odd fellow is the one-to-one relationship. Between object types and their properties there are always one-to-one relationships, also known as *dependencies*. But one-to-one relationships do happen between business object types. Not that often, however. The examples all tend to be more in the business rules space than in the data model realm. Figure 8-10 shows one, which we have seen before.

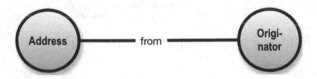

Figure 8-10.   Only one from originator

Having only one "from" address per originator seems to me to be a business decision made in the the legacy design of Internet email messages. A message where the originator is a group of "from" addresses is perfectly conceivable.

However, it is worth checking whether the relationship is information bearing. That could be the case, like in the previous example. It is conceivable that "in reply to" carries a date, and that the resulting API design should be different.

This, by the way, once again confirms the assumption that most of the time many-to-many relationships are information bearing constructs.

In general, both nodes and relationships can (should) have "names" (formally called labels for nodes and types for relationships), just like concepts and their relationships have in Figure 8-10.

Relationships are directed, which is visualized by the arrowheads.

Both nodes and relationships may be associated with properties, which are key/value pairs, such as Color:Red. On the data model level, we call the key a property name.

Note   The labeled property graph model is the most flexible general purpose data model paradigm that we have today.

The important things are the names and the structure (the nodes and the relationships). The properties supplement the solution structure by way of adding content. Properties are also basically just labels, but they can signify "identity" (the general idea of a key on the data model level).

Finally, self-references are also visiting data models from time to time. Figure 8-11 shows a double example. Messages may refer to another message, either in reference to or in reply to.

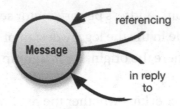

Figure 8-11. *Two self-references*

When you later traverse such self-references with a GraphQL query, you should understand the resulting tree structure. It is probably best to use GraphiQL[5] to get a feel for it, by playing with the schema.

You should also be quite certain that a self-reference is not really information bearing in any way. Quite frequently relationships like that carry a start date and an end date. This could call for a separate little object type, having a name that reflects the periodicity of the relationship, having the two dates as properties. More about this on the resolver level in a later chapter.

Are you struggling with understanding data structures? Draw a little property graph—that will help!

Good Relationships

Relationships are key to getting the structure right. Even simple (one-to-many) relationships have some considerations. Part of the idea of using concepts and relationships analysis is that you should pay attention to *the linking phrase* between concepts (the label on the relationship arrow). If you get those names right, the structure and meaning are bound to be more correct.

---

[5]https://github.com/graphql/graphiql

Look at the property graph (with named relationships) in Figure 8-12.

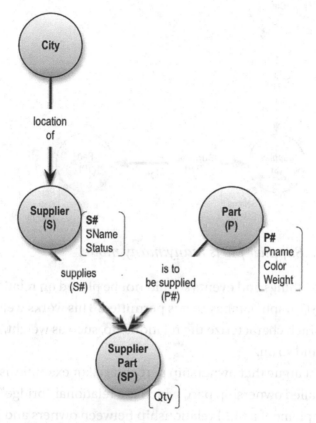

Figure 8-12. *Named relationships*

Good, inter-object relationships are based on action verbs. In this example, the verbs represent localization (City is the location of Supplier) and supply chain (Supplier supplies SupplierPart and Part is to be supplied by SupplierPart). SupplierPart is really an instance of a many-to-many relationship between Suppliers and Parts. The name SupplierPart seems a bit constructed and not really coming straight from business terminology. The challenge is that we have information on the relationship. SupplierPart carries a Qty (and in reality at least a date of the supply). Figure 8-13 shows it as a many-to-many design.

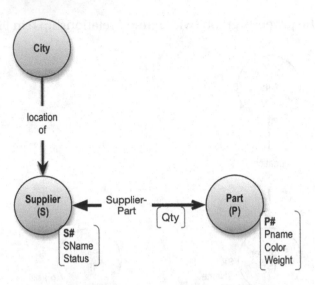

Figure 8-13. *Supplier parts many:many model*

In general, things and events should not be placed on relationships. In some (most) graph databases, it is permitted. This works well with properties, which characterize the relationship, such as weight, ownership percentage, and so on.

One might argue that ownership percentage, for example, is a property of an entity called ownership part, which is a relational "bridge" table helping to implement a M:M relationship between owners and properties. This is mostly a business decision. If the business folks do not recognize the concept of an ownership part, the story ends there.

Frequently (not always), a "bridging thing" can be named, and it will, most often, carry information, as in the supplier-parts example. Be careful here—constructed object types must have meaningful names and definitions, which the business can relate to. On the other hand, if you do not have a graph database, you are forced (at least in SQL) to materialize the "bridge table" and place the information owned by the relationship there.

In graph database sources, M:M is perfectly fine. We discuss that in the resolver discussions later.

What are the consequences for the GraphQL API? The results are tree structures. In the simple supplier parts example, there are basically two ways the tree can be constructed, as shown in Figure 8-14.

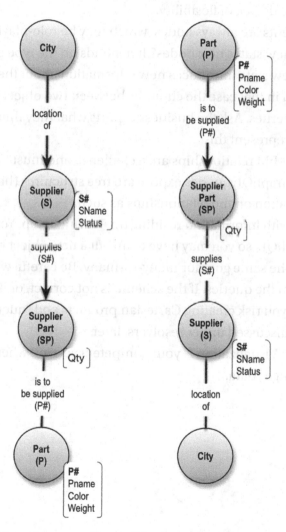

Figure 8-14. *Supplier parts possible trees*

The question is, which resolver function should produce the information on the M:M relationship? In this case it is QTY, and it can be produced either together with `Supplier` or together with `Part`. That is not very flexible across the board. It you choose to materialize the M:M `SupplierPart` as an object type of its own at the schema level, you have the highest possible degree of flexibility.

Objects/events are always nodes, which may be role-playing and state-changing. Are new states new nodes? It depends on the type of business. Sometimes a new state introduces new information about the object type/event, and in that case the choice is between two object types versus additional properties. Ask the business experts what they think is the most natural way to represent this.

In general, M:M relationships are a challenge and must be handled, because what GraphQL queries expose are tree structures (hierarchical) with no information on the relationships as such.

Be careful with information residing on a relationship. You cannot do that in GraphQL, so you may have to invent a new object type for that purpose. The same goes for many-to-many. Be careful when you traverse them in the queries. If the schema is not correct, or if the data has redundancies, you risk creating Cartesian products and "queries from hell". This is further discussed under resolvers, later.

Remember: Visualization is your competent servant when you're exploring "strange" data.

CHAPTER 9

From Graph to Trees

Structure Design at the API Level

The schema definitions are on the server side. What you see at the application side is being exposed as a result of the schema design.

The GraphQL list modifier is an easy way to generate a sub-branch of the result tree. In our Email example, we have plenty of lists. For example, the keywords tagging a message:

```
keywords: [Keyword] @relation(name: "Tags")
```

Lists can handle nulls, which are syntactically visualized in GraphQL:

- The data can be null: [Keyword]

- The data cannot be null: [Keyword!]

- The list cannot be null: [Keyword!]!

Another GraphQL construct that can be useful in complex situations is the *union*.

Remember the design challenge about contacts having interfaces versus not having a contact as a type? Unions can help build a consolidated list of contacts (originators and destinations):

```
Union Contacts = Originator | Destination
```

© Thomas Frisendal 2018
T. Frisendal, *Visual Design of GraphQL Data*,
https://doi.org/10.1007/978-1-4842-3904-9_9

However, since the contributing object types may not be completely compatible, you may need to use inline fragments in the query:

```
 1   {
 2     SearchResult {
 3       ... on Originator {
 4         origin_date
 5       }
 6       ... on Destination {
 7         received_date
 8       }
 9     }
10   }
```

Refer to the GraphQL documentation[1] at http://graphql.org/learn/ for more information.

In the context of this book, you must remember that we are building a scope for result trees sharing a root query (per schema) in the GraphQL API.

---

[1]http://graphql.org/learn/

Positioning the Graph for Generation of Trees

Figure 9-1 shows the email data model from before.

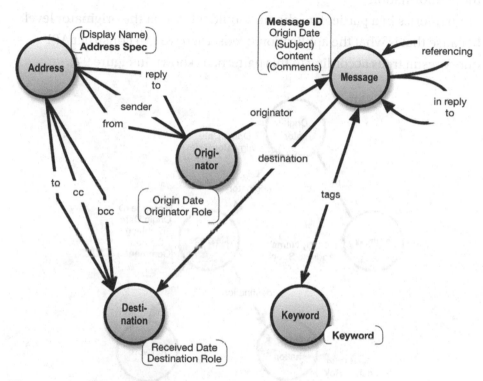

Figure 9-1. *Our email property graph once again*

This data model is a directed graph, and it can be traversed in any direction (using graph technologies, but not GraphQL). GraphQL must result in a tree for each and every *query*.

Note that the graph shown in Figure 9-2 is also a property graph—now just a "Banzai" version of the schema graph, and a twisted one at that.

Much depends on what your root query looks like. It determines the perspective of the possible queries. A schema should be serving a particular application's needs.

You can have multiple fields in your root query. You can also have multiple schemas in your configuration. The schema-stitching possibility enables you to merge schemas, essentially bringing the root fields together in the combined root query. Refer to the GraphQL documentation for more information.

If queries in a particular schema should all start at the originator level, because that is what the application needs, then we can construct API query result trees according to this pattern, as shown in Figure 9-2.

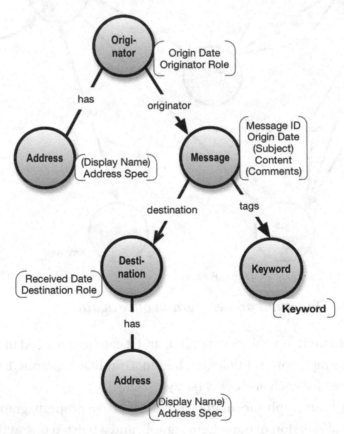

Figure 9-2. *Having originator as the root of a query*

This implies that address-level or keyword-level properties, for example, will be redundantly available in the trees, since they must be denormalized into a lower level or, alternatively, into a GraphQL list construct.

Property graphs are highly relevant to GraphQL developers. They ease the analysis of the data at hand significantly, and they help organize the resulting API schema and query structures.

Having done this, we have also dealt with:

- Correct exposure of the structure of the relationships inherent in the exposed data (query result).

- Handling traversals of many-to-many relationships in order to produce a result tree (both schema and query result).

The visualization is an intuitively understandable (pretty good) representation of business and application terminology that can be discussed with business folks.

An easy way to get an overview of the query scope is to turn and twist the application graph data model so that it visualizes the result tree scope in a top-down, left-to-right manner (see Figure 9-3).

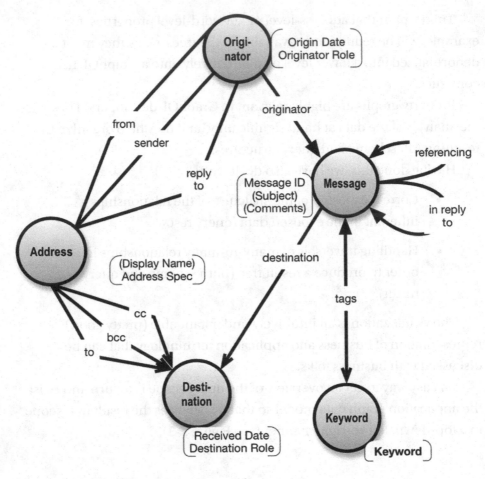

Figure 9-3. *Pulling originator to the top*

Note that a branch of the tree can traverse the M:M relationship in one direction only.

If another application perspective should be on messages with certain tags sent by someone to certain destinations, the result tree visualization could look like Figure 9-4.

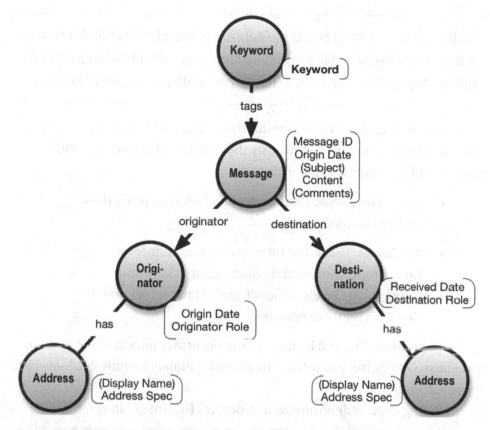

Figure 9-4. Result tree having keyword as root

The tree, which can be derived, is rooted in the keyword and will deliver, keyword after keyword, all the messages having been tagged with that keyword. For each such message, all originators will be listed with their respective addresses and all destinations.

Navigating the graph data model can also be eased by way of visually "lassoing" individual sub-trees (hierarchies). This will give you a feel for which result trees can be constructed.

In other words, denormalization and duplication are your good friends. In the case of GraphQL, the data lives in the API, i.e., in the cache at runtime.

Note   One the strong points of GraphQL is based on just that: Having a tree-structure carefully self-defined and available in the caches of a distributed application leads to better performance and less blocking.

So, no problems in exposing redundant data, and for some physical data stores, it is a necessity. Obviously the tree-based denormalization result could contain the following:

- *Data*: The selected leaf-node data (selected properties in the schema design).

- *Navigation fields*: The intermediate and top-level node properties, which include identity keys and intermediate levels of classification hierarchies and the like. This is for convenience.

It is important that you include all the necessary intermediate and top-level keys. Otherwise, you will not be able to uniquely identify each level in the result.

Mapping already denormalized structures (in NoSQL stores, for example) to GraphQL should normally be possible and relatively easy to do in most cases, but changing the serialization order is not for the faint-hearted.

You can also consider using repeating groups of columns. Sometimes there are not too many in a 1:M relationship, so repeating fields could work well and are supported by GraphQL lists.

In general, mapping from a solution data model expressed as a graph to query results expressed as trees is pretty straightforward. Your visualizations will help you get good at doing that, which you will appreciate once your schema graph is large.

Producing correct result trees is a big part of the resolver requirements, which is what we look at in the next chapter.

CHAPTER 10

Resolving Legacy SQL Data Issues

Using GraphQL with a new, empty data store is the easy way. In many cases, the database schema and resolvers (if needed) can be generated or inferred from the GraphQL schema.

If you plan to use GraphQL with existing databases, you should mind your steps, as illustrated in Figure 10-1.

© Thomas Frisendal 2018
T. Frisendal, *Visual Design of GraphQL Data*,
https://doi.org/10.1007/978-1-4842-3904-9_10

Figure 10-1. *The bridge to GraphQL crossing river legacy*

Having been active in the data warehouse community for years, I know the SQL database "jungle" well. Applying GraphQL to this bewildering legacy of SQL data is the context for this chapter. Expect some surprises as you cross the bridge.

There are additional tools you may use, such as:

- Object-relational mappers (ORMs) (such as Sequelize at http://docs.sequelizejs.com/, for example[1])

- SQL generators (such as join-monster, at https:// github.com/stems/join-monster/blob/master/ README.md for example[2])

I do not have practical experience with any of them; you will have to build your own. Both of them look good from their websites, and they do have some customers. I am bit skeptical about the ORMs. Seems to me that you have to build another schema, just for the sake of the mapping. That can potentially amount to quite a few hours spent, I think.

In the following example, I expect that your platform can build resolver functions, which can contain or issue (almost unrestricted) SQL commands.

Let's walk through the specific legacy issues in the same order as we presented the general issues earlier.

Data Names

More often than not, you will have to map the physical column and table names to the business facing terminology of the GraphQL types. This is annoying and takes some time.

Wait! Maybe somebody has already done parts of that work? It could be in reporting or data warehouse contexts, and it could be SQL views and/ or ETL-jobs that contain the mappings. Look around. I am a fan of SQL views, so if you need the mapping, do it in views, which are reusable. If the underlying database schema changes, you can, to some extent, continue

---

[1]http://docs.sequelizejs.com
[2]https://github.com/stems/join-monster/blob/master/README.md

to support the views' result sets without impacting the GraphQL schemas. Using views may also give you a better opportunity to exploit "automatic mapping" between GraphQL and the source views.

Using Select * is not a good idea, because data models do change, and they are typically extended with new columns and occasional changes in physical data types. So this is actually another good argument for using views to insulate your API even more from the physical data.

Identity, Uniqueness, and Keys

Note   Many SQL database designs include system-generated keys of the surrogate key kind. These can most likely be reused as Xxxxxx ID identity fields in your API design, which is good. The scope of such keys is typically at the database instance level, but the surrogate keys may have been carried over into data warehouse tables and the like. GraphQL supports "ID" as a scalar type. The scope of such a GraphQL ID field is within that object type within that application (server), and the ID is mainly for getting data out of the cache. They are unique within that scope, but not more than that.

Uniqueness in the databases is not controlled in the same way as the business-level uniqueness rules are defined. Typically a row in a table should be unique across several components in a concatenated string of business keys. The keys, in turn, frequently represent a hierarchy such as Customer/Order/Orderline/Product and more.

Identity is the matter of what controls the uniqueness in the database. Most often it is a single "surrogate key" field guaranteeing the uniqueness of the orderline, for example. In principle, surrogate keys should not carry information other than the identity of the row. But that is not always the case.

In mainstream data modeling the last 20-30 years, the use of surrogate keys is widespread. Clever people have added another purpose to them: The issue of identifying the nonexistent! (I am not going to get into a SQL NULL-discussion, because SQL NULLs are generally no good.) What many applications nowadays rely on is that the ID (the key) equaling 0 (zero, not null) is the representation of the nonexistent instance at the other end of the join. That means, of course, that there should exist a row in the database table referred to in the join, which has "Id" = 0. Those rows typically contain default values. The issue here is to avoid the use of SQL outer joins, which would otherwise be required. Look out for "zero records". See Figure 10-2.

CustomerID	FirstName	LastName	FullName
0	Not specified	Not specified	Not specified
291	Gustavo	Achong	Gustavo Achong
293	Catherine	Abel	Catherine Abel
295	Kim	Abercrombie	Kim Abercrombie
297	Humberto	Acevedo	Humberto Acevedo
299	Pilar	Ackerman	Pilar Ackerman
301	Frances	Adams	Frances Adams
303	Margaret	Smith	Margaret Smith
305	Carla	Adams	Carla Adams
307	Jay	Adams	Jay Adams
309	Ronald	Adina	Ronald Adina
311	Samuel	Agcaoili	Samuel Agcaoili
313	James	Aguilar	James Aguilar
315	Robert	Ahlering	Robert Ahlering

Figure 10-2. *A first in class zero record*

If there is no surrogate key in a table, then the primary key must be examined. Often primary keys are information bearing, which is to be avoided. Even social security numbers and the ilk may change over time. Some item numbers may be reused after some time of inactivity and so forth.

Using a GraphQL schema directive might be a good way to generate globally unique object identifiers, if you need to do so.

States, Versions, and Housekeeping

States (business states, for example Planned, Ordered, Delivered, and Archived) are not always modeled explicitly in elderly data models. They can be rather easy to generate by way of a SQL CASE construct, either in a resolver function or in an underlying view. Business people love them because they are looking for state information all the time.

Versions are the same story, really. Ideally, most business needs can be met with the simple construct of three new concepts:

- Valid From Date (could be 1900-01-01 for unknown historic dates)

- Valid To Date (could be 2099-12-31 for unknown future dates)

- Current Version (a flag string containing "Yes" or "No" for example).

But, if the legacy data are not persisted with versions, you will have to look for old versions in a data warehouse or a data vault database. If they are not there, you cannot satisfy that business need without further ado. If you can get the funding for that, you could look at time series paradigms, including key/value stores and graph databases for solving the persistence of versioned data.

Other housekeeping data can include (where applicable):

- UserId of the user who created the record

- CreationDate of the record

- UserId of the user who changed this record the last time

- `ChangeTimeStamp` of the date and time of the last change

- Identification of the batch process that loaded this record

- `LoadTimeStamp` when the record was loaded

- Name of the source system of the record (if this record is not the golden record)

- And more

Look for states, versions, and other housekeeping data in the reporting and data warehouse parts of your organization. Somebody may have done the hard work already.

Scalar Data Types

The type system of GraphQL is meant to be coercive, and the server will do its best to deliver according to the specified data type in the schema. That could involve truncating a floating point value to an integer value, if that is what it takes to stay "within the contract". But there will still be a need for transformations at the resolver level. Check your data.

Another issue is the matter of "prettifying" your data. A three-digit integer can be a product category code, but it must be accompanied by a textual description. Many users will not know the code values by heart.

The GraphQL type system is extensible in the newest working draft of the GraphQL schema specification. It is going to be interesting to see how it develops in the next year or so.

Date and Time

IT has struggled with date and time since the 1960s.

Let's start at the bottom. Date and time are mixed into a variety of data types in many data stores and DBMS products. Some of the types can be:

- Pure date

- Date and time in one property

- Time in its own property

Be careful about which server you pull the date and time information. Much depends on the settings of those servers and database instances.

Another issue is handling missing dates. If you want to avoid SQL_NULLs (and who doesn't?), you could define default low and high dates, which are supplied whenever a date (or time-of-day) is missing. Sometimes we record future dates on records, which have happened now, but where the future event is still to happen in a couple of years' time (budgets, for example). Not very elegant modeling, but it happens. You may end up having to define a "future undefined date" (a default high date that you choose).

In the data warehousing world, a date/calendar dimension is a given requirement. But for the same reasons as the reporting and analytics need to know about calendars (such as public holidays or banking days), ordinary applications need to keep track of several properties of dates and sometimes also of time of days. Be prepared.

Naming Relationships

As pointed out earlier in this book, the relationship names are important for conveying the meaning of the structure of the data. So, at the GraphQL Schema level, I recommend that you use the Graphcool @relation directive to convey that structural information.

At the resolver level, you have the job of figuring out how to do a join that satisfies the relationship. This could be a foreign key constraint (if you are lucky). It could also be two columns in two distinct tables with the same name. Or it could be inferred from an index on the target table (one or more columns). Or, you just either have to know or you have to use data profiling to find inter-table dependencies in the data.

Relationship Types
One-to-One Relationships

These are sometimes one-to-none relationships and sometimes one-to-one. In the first case, the default properties of the missing instance should be handled by the resolver. There are normally good business reasons for maintaining the divide between the two, and if the resolver can produce that, then that is what you must do.

One/Zero to Zero/Many Relationships

Again, if the relationship is empty (for example, a customer without orders), the tree stops here. I think it might be prettier to stop with "Not available" instead of nothing (a null).

Self References

Let's take the example of Manager is and Manages (the view from the manager side).

- Manager is is a one-to-one relationship where the upper end may be empty (employees without a manager).

- Manages is a one/zero to zero/many relationship (remember that a manager may not have any employees at this time, and no, this does not support matrix organizations).

Depending on the root, you may have to generate redundant data for the Manager is relationship.

Many-to-Many Relationships

This is where you need a large cache. You have to duplicate redundant information such that the tree structure of the result set is maintained. Recall the supplier/parts, as shown in Figure 10-3.

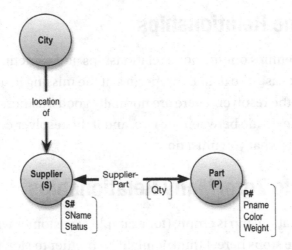

***Figure 10-3.** Supplier/parts many:many model*

What are the consequences for the GraphQL API? The results are tree structures. In the simple supplier parts example, there are basically two ways the tree can be constructed, as shown in Figure 10-4.

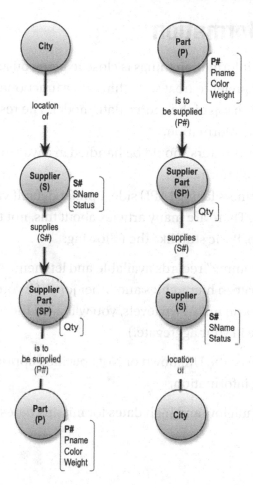

Figure 10-4. *Supplier parts possible trees*

The question is, which resolver function should produce the information on the M:M relationship?

In this case it is QTY, and it can be produced together with Supplier or together with Part. That is not very flexible across the board. If you choose to materialize the M:M SupplierPart as an object type of its own at the schema level, you have the highest possible degree of flexibility.

Missing Information

Handling missing information things is close to being business rules driven. I generally prefer to treat such things in a functional layer (like a resolver function) on top of the source data model. The resolvers need to resolve the missing information.

At this level, the matters should be handled in a way that matches the capabilities of the platform.

But on the business facing (API) side, I prefer default value schemes over using NULLs. There are many articles about this, not the least from the Kimball Group. Basic stuff like the following:

- Keep "dummy" records available and let them participate in hierarchies and other joins. (If you report numbers on unknown levels, you will need the Unknown instance in your aggregate.)

- Use at least the Unknown or Not Specified approach for missing information.

- Use default low and high dates for missing dates.

- Etc.

Properties on Relationships

This is not supported in SQL. The closest thing is a helper/bridge table, which should also materialize as a type on the GraphQL level.

CHAPTER 11

Using GraphQL with an Existing Graph Database

It is of course a relevant question to ask that, since GraphQL is based on graph thinking, how can we use GraphQL on top of a graph database? To answer that, we first look at the use case in which an existing graph database is supported from a GraphQL API. Later we look at a common use case, whereby a GraphQL API will be used with a new graph database.

Since transformations are based on the language of the DBMS, I use the language of the Neo4j[1] graph platform (see https://neo4j.com/). It is called Cypher, and it is a very powerful, declarative language. While Neo4j uses Cypher, the language has been open sourced through the openCypher project and there are now a number of other projects using Cypher[2] (see http://www.opencypher.org/).

---

[1] https://neo4j.com
[2] http://www.opencypher.org

© Thomas Frisendal 2018
T. Frisendal, *Visual Design of GraphQL Data*,
https://doi.org/10.1007/978-1-4842-3904-9_11

The Neo4j GraphQL Plugin

Neo4j has done a great job of integrating GraphQL into the Neo4j platform. The easiest way to use it is to use a plugin installed in the Neo4j Desktop interface.

Will Lyon (working in developer relations at Neo4j) has made an excellent video explaining everything. It's called "Using The Neo4j-GraphQL Plugin With Neo4j Desktop"[3] (see `https://youtu.be/J-J9Ouwugb4`).

Basically the plugin enables you to serve a GraphQL endpoint directly from Neo4j by:

- Generating a GraphQL schema from existing Neo4j data

- Serving a GraphQL endpoint based on a GraphQL schema that you supply

- Translating GraphQL to Cypher (on the fly)

- Automatically generating query types for querying with GraphQL

- Automatically generating mutation types for write operations from GraphQL

- Exposing Cypher through GraphQL as a `@cypher` schema directive

You can also find more information about the plugin in Will Lyon's blog post called "Using The Neo4j-GraphQL Plugin In Neo4j Desktop"[4] (see `https://blog.grandstack.io/using-the-neo4j-graphql-plugin-in-neo4j-desktop-c8a60aa014d9`).

---

[3]`https://youtu.be/J-J9Ouwugb4`

[4]`https://blog.grandstack.io/using-the-neo4j-graphql-plugin-in-neo4j-desktop-c8a60aa014d9`

Generating Your First GraphQL Schema

It really is very simple. You install the plugin from the Neo4j Desktop, as shown in Figure 11-1.

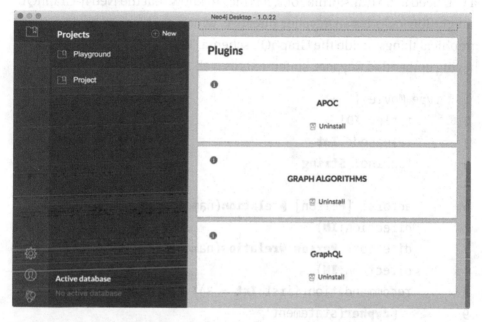

Figure 11-1. Plugin installation from the Neo4j Desktop

Having installed the plugin, you will want to install the Electron version of the GraphiQL app[5] for browsing and testing. Refer to the video and the blog post for details about setting up the endpoint and authorization headers to make the connection (not a big deal).

To generate the schema from the data in the Neo4j database, issue this command to the Neo4j Desktop:

```
CALL graphql.idl(null);
```

---

[5]https://electronjs.org/apps/graphiql

You may have to transform the existing data to make it fit for presentation through GraphQL. This depends on the quality of the data and likewise of the metadata (labels, property names, and relationship types). In the following sections, we will go through the potential issues. If you need to do transformations, it is nice to know that the Neo4j-GraphQL integration includes an @cypher directive, which enables you to do some graphical things inside the GraphQL schema. Take a look at this example having embedded @cypher statements as well as type extensions:

```
1    type Movie {
2        title: ID!
3        released: Int
4        tagline: String
5
6        actors: [Person] @relation(name:"ACTED_IN",
         direction:IN)
7        director: Person @relation(name:"DIRECTED",
         direction:IN)
8        recommendation(first:Int = 3): [Movie]
9          @cypher(statement:
10           "MATCH (this)<-[r1:REVIEWED]-(:User)-
             [r2:REVIEWED]->(reco:Movie)
11                             WHERE 3 <= r1.stars <= r2.stars
12                             RETURN reco, sum(r2.stars) as
                               rating
13                             ORDER BY rating DESC")
14   }
15   interface Person {
16       name: ID!
17       born: Int
18   }
19   type Actor extends Person {
```

```
20        name: ID!
21        born: Int
22
23        movies: [Movie] @relation(name:"ACTED_IN")
24    }
25    type Director extends Person {
26        name: ID!
27        born: Int
28
29        movies: [Movie] @relation(name:"DIRECTED")
30    }
31    type Mutations {
32        directed(movie:ID! director:ID!) : String
33          @cypher(statement:
34            "MATCH (m:Movie {title: $movie}), (d:Person {name:
                 $director})
35                  MERGE (d)-[.DIRECTED]->(m)")
36    }
37    schema {
38      mutations: Mutations
39    }
```

Note that fields annotated with the @cypher schema directive then become "computed" fields. This technique allows for some transformation between how the data is stored in Neo4j and how it is presented in the GraphQL layer.

The video and the blog post cited in this chapter cover the how-tos of using GraphQL on top of an existing graph database, as well as on top of a blank graph database, which is the last subject of this book.

Let's recast the legacy SQL issues and see how they apply in the context of an existing Neo4j database.

Data Names

The Neo4j-GraphQL plugin will derive a GraphQL schema from the existing graph data. By way of sampling, the integration adds a type for each Node-Label with all the properties and their types found as fields.

This gives you a much better starting point than a blank slate. However, much depends on the quality of the existing data model, of course. So, being a bit cynical, you should expect to spend some time on mapping not-so-good names to something business facing. The mapping will be done by way of editing the generated GraphQL schema, e.g., @cypher extensions. Just as with SQL, you may spend time here, but the time spent should be less than what would need to be done in SQL. Some SQL databases that I have seen almost needed an archeologist in order to establish data identities.

Identity, Uniqueness, and Keys

Neo4j can live without constraints, but you can also have them. Data profiling[6] (see https://neo4j.com/blog/data-profiling-holistic-view-neo4j/) is rather easy, and you should spend some time double-checking candidate keys. So, just as with SQL, you may have to spend some time here.

The Neo4j node ID is internal use only. Don't use internal Neo4j IDs for long-term entity identification. Future versions of Neo4j might shift these IDs around for performance purposes. Create your own unique ID property (ideally with a *constraint*) for tracking entities.

States, Versions, and Housekeeping

As with SQL, you might want to spend some time here. One benefit, though: Neo4j is schema-free, so refactoring the database is much easier than in SQL.

---

[6]https://neo4j.com/blog/data-profiling-holistic-view-neo4j/

Scalar Data Types

Neo4j does not have explicit types, but the Neo4j-GraphQL is coercive, and the proper types will be transmitted by default in most cases. Type conversion functions are available, though. There might be issues with string-encoded information, which should be something else (a float, for example). This may take some time to identify and fix.

Date and Time

Neo4j does not have any date and time types per se. However, in Neo4j 3.x, APOC procedure support was added, including procedures for date/time support[7] (see https://neo4j-contrib.github.io/neo4j-apoc-procedures/#_date_and_time_conversions). This enables you to handle most conversions from Cypher commands.

Support of temporal functions in Cypher per se arrived in release 3.4.

GraphAware has a library called TimeTree[8], which looks interesting, as shown in Figure 11-2. See https://graphaware.com/neo4j/2014/08/20/graphaware-neo4j-timetree.html.

---

[7]https://neo4j-contrib.github.io/neo4j-apoc-procedures/#_date_and_time_conversions

[8]https://graphaware.com/neo4j/2014/08/20/graphaware-neo4j-timetree.html

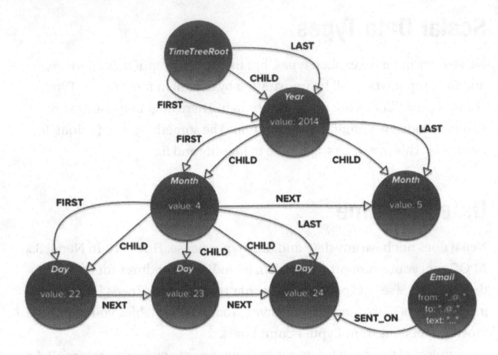

Figure 11-2. *TimeTree from GraphAware*

Naming Relationships

The Neo4j-GraphQL plugin[9] will generate GraphQL schema code using the `@relation` directive. It looks like this for the `ACTED_IN` relationship in the Movie database:

```
1    type Person { name: String, movies : Movie @relation
     (name:"ACTED_IN", direction:OUT)\
2    }
```

[9]https://github.com/neo4j-graphql/neo4j-graphql#schema-from-graph

As you can see, the Neo4j-GraphQL plugin uses the `@relation` directive to encode a relationship type, but also a direction since graphs are directed in the property graph model.

Again, the quality (business-facing) of the relationship type names will depend on whodunnit.

Relationship Types

The Neo4j-GraphQL integration will catch most of what you need.

In a Neo4j graph database, M:M is perfectly fine. However, you will have to split them into two. If you recall in the Movie example, there is a M:M in the ACTED_IN relationship. That will give you two relationships (@relation in GraphQL):

- Movies are the movies that an Actor acted in

- Actors lists the actors in a Movie

You can easily check the cardinalities in Cypher:

```
1   MATCH (p:Person)-[:WROTE]->(m)<-[:WROTE]-(coPersons:Person)
2   RETURN p, m, coPersons
```

The path query returns some data, which shows that even the WROTE relationship (and, as it happens, the DIRECTED relationship) is many-to-many, as shown in Figure 11-3.

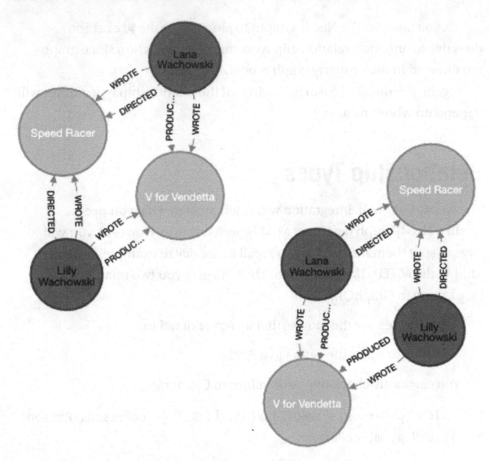

Figure 11-3. *Finding many to many*

The data is just for demo purposes. Obviously, in real life, there are many more cases like these of M:M relationships in the movie context.

Missing Information

Missing information is handled differently in Neo4j when compared to SQL. In SQL you use NULL values, but in Neo4j (and most other NoSQL data types), missing information is simply not there. Take the age of a person, for example. Age is a property, and if a Person node has no known age, the Age property is missing on that node.

In GraphQL on the user-facing side, you can have non-nullable fields, which means that you may have to handle the generation of default values yourself. Fortunately the @cypher extension can be used for that, as shown in the sample GraphQL schema.

I do think that NULLs should be avoided and that they can be replaced by default values according to business specifications.

Properties on Relationships

In my honest opinion, things and events should not be placed on relationships. In some (most) graph databases, it is permitted. However, it works well with properties, which characterize the relationship, such as weight, ownership percentage, and so on.

One might argue that ownership percentage, for example, is a property of an entity called ownership share, which is a relational bridge table helping to implement a M:M relationship between owners and properties. This is mostly a business decision. If the business folks do not recognize the concept of an ownership share, the story ends there.

If the introduction of a new business level concept like ownership share is acceptable, then the relationship surfaces as a new GraphQL object type having a scalar field representing the percentage. Two new relationships will emerge. The API designer will have to decide the traversal path, obviously. Given that the restriction is on the GraphQL concepts side, this is an acceptable solution.

CHAPTER 12

Using GraphQL with a New Graph Database

Design Goals of the Neo4j-GraphQL Integration

What does a graph solution for a GraphQL API look like?

I can best answer this question by looking at the Neo4j-GraphQL plugin. Instead of repeating what Will Lyon says in his video, I have decided to briefly summarize a recent blog post from March 2018, also by Will Lyon of Neo4j. It's entitled "Five Common GraphQL Problems and How Neo4j-GraphQL Aims To Solve Them[1]" (see https://blog. grandstack.io/five-common-graphql-problems-and-how-neo4j-graphql-aims-to-solve-them-e9a8999c8d43).

---

[1]https://blog.grandstack.io/five-common-graphql-problems-and-how-neo4j-graphql-aims-to-solve-them-e9a8999c8d43

Obviously, there are advantages to using a graph database as a store for a GraphQL API, as you will see. In the following, Will explains the ambitions of the GraphQL Neo4j integration:

> A few weeks ago, I came across an article from Sacha Greif[2] on freeCodeCamp titled "Five Common Problems in GraphQL Apps (And How to Fix Them)".[3] I thought this was a good overview of some of problems developers encounter when adopting GraphQL.
>
> As I read through the list of common problems, I realized these were some of the same issues that users had complained about when we were researching how a Neo4j-GraphQL integration would look[4] (see `https://neo4j.com/developer/graphql/`). Ultimately, the design of our integration aimed to help developers be more productive when building GraphQL services backed by Neo4j.
>
> In this post, I would like to revisit each of the five problems that Sacha points out and show how Neo4j-GraphQL addresses each of those issues.

---

[2]`https://medium.com/@sachagreif`

[3]`https://medium.freecodecamp.org/five-common-problems-in-graphql-apps-and-how-to-fix-them-ac74d37a293c`

[4]`https://neo4j.com/developer/graphql/`

Problem 1: Schema Duplication

Namely, you need one schema for your database, and another one for your GraphQL endpoint. —Sacha Greif

GraphQL uses a strictly defined schema, which defines the types available and the entry points for the API. This schema acts as the specification for the GraphQL API, and with introspection enables powerful developer tools such as query completion, mocking, and documentation generation. However, standard GraphQL implementations often require working with a schema for your database and a schema for your GraphQL API.

To simplify the process of building GraphQL applications backed by Neo4j, the Neo4j-GraphQL integration uses the GraphQL schema to infer what the Neo4j data model should be.

Solution: Use the GraphQL schema to drive the Neo4j database model.

Problem 2: Server/Client Data Mismatch

Your database and GraphQL API will have different schemas, which translate into different document shapes. —Sacha Greif

If the backend for your GraphQL service is not a graph database, then there is some mapping and translation that must occur to transform the data from how you model it at the data persistence layer to the shape of a graph for GraphQL. By using a graph database as the data layer for our GraphQL service, we preempt this problem.

The Neo4j-GraphQL integration translates any arbitrary GraphQL request to Cypher,[5] the query language for graphs, and handles the database call as part of the GraphQL resolver.

Solution: Translate GraphQL to Cypher. (Note: This is done automatically.)

Problem 3: Superfluous Database Calls

Imagine a list of posts, each of which has a user attached to it. You now want to display 10 of these posts, along with the name of their author. —Sacha Greif

As Sacha points out, for the example above, a typical GraphQL implementation makes one database query for the list of posts, then one query per post to fetch the user. This results in 11 round-trip requests to the database! This is known as the n+1 query problem and the common solution is to use a tool like Dataloader.

We can certainly use Dataloader[6] with Neo4j—it is designed to be data layer agnostic, but with Neo4j-GraphQL we have the advantage of generating a *single* Cypher query for any arbitrary GraphQL request. This means for any GraphQL request we make only a single request to the database.

Solution: Translate GraphQL to a single Cypher query. (Note: This is done automatically.)

---

[5]http://www.opencypher.org
[6]https://github.com/facebook/dataloader

Problem 4: Poor Performance

On one hand you want to take full advantage of GraphQL's graph traversal features ("show me the authors of the comments of the author of the post of ..." etc.). But on the other hand, you don't want your app to become slow and unresponsive. —Sacha Greif

While it is true that GraphQL enables the expression of graph traversals like the example above, many of the database systems responsible for resolving the data are not optimized for these workloads. Graph databases like Neo4j are optimized for graph traversal queries like this. By translating GraphQL to Cypher, we can take advantage of the powerful performance benefits of using a graph database execution engine like Neo4j. Furthermore, GraphQL lacks the semantics of a database query language for expressing things like filtering, projects, or aggregations. Through the use of GraphQL schema directives, we can use the power of Cypher with GraphQL to map a GraphQL field to the result of an arbitrary Cypher query.

Solution: Expose the power of Cypher in GraphQL.

Problem 5: Boilerplate Overdose

This is by no means an issue exclusive to GraphQL apps, but it's true that they generally require you to write a lot of similar boilerplate code. —Sacha Greif

Implementing a typical GraphQL service involves writing a schema for the GraphQL service, a schema for the database, resolver functions to fetch the data, AND mutations for creating and updating data. Much of this is boilerplate code that can be generated by inspecting the GraphQL schema.

Solution: Auto-generate Query and Mutation types from GraphQL schema. See Figure 12-1.

We mentioned previously that resolvers are implemented automatically by inferring the database schema from the GraphQL schema, translating GraphQL to Cypher, and handling the database call. Additionally, the entry points for the GraphQL service (Query and Mutation types) are auto-generated as well, reducing the boilerplate code necessary to implement a GraphQL service backed by Neo4j. In addition, first, offset, filter-fields, ordering for both top-level queries and fields pointing to other entities are generated.

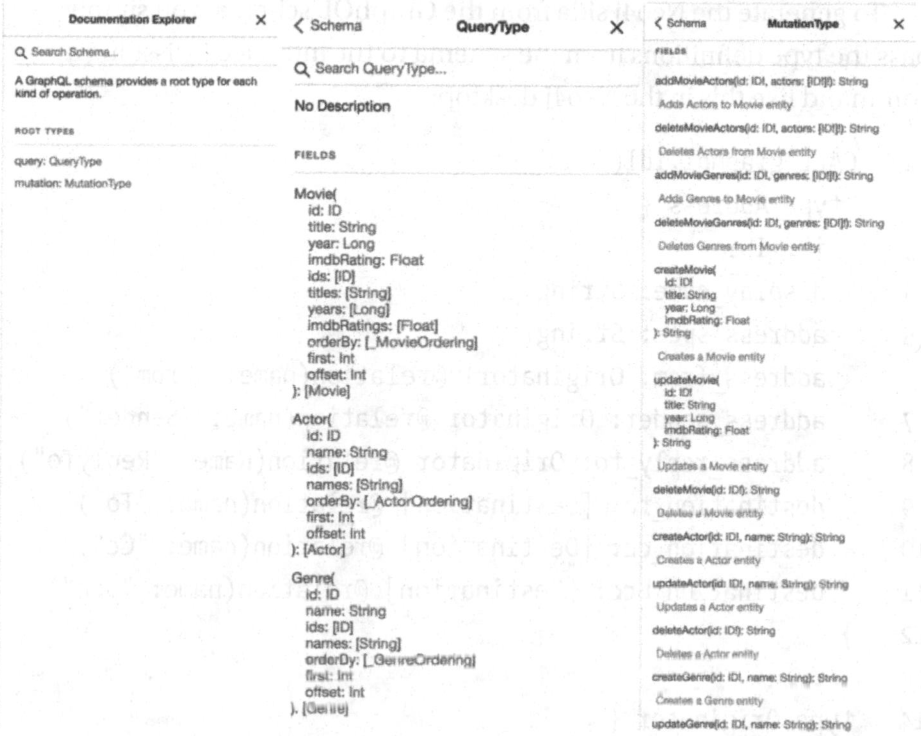

Figure 12-1. *Query and Mutation types are generated automatically when using Neo4j-GraphQL*

This concludes the post by Will Lyon about the design goals of Neo4j-GraphQL.

Let's see it in action!

Generating Your Neo4j Database from the GraphQL Schema

Let's use the email example, which I introduced in earlier chapters of this book, in Neo4j.

To generate the Neo4j side from the GraphQL schema, you simply
pass the type definitions from the schema to the interface by issuing a
command like this in the Neo4j desktop:

```
1    CALL graphql.idl(
2    'type Address {
3      id: ID!
4      display_name: String
5      address_spec: String!
6      address_from: Originator! @relation(name: "From")
7      address_sender: Originator @relation(name: "Sender")
8      address_reply_to: Originator @relation(name: "ReplyTo")
9      destination_to: [Destination] @relation(name: "To")
10     destination_cc: [Destination] @relation(name: "Cc")
11     destination_bcc: [Destination] @relation(name: "Bcc")
12   }
13
14   type Originator {
15     id: ID!
16     origin_date: String!
17     originator_role: String!
18     message: [Message!] @relation(name: "Originator")
19     address_from: Address! @relation(name: "From",
         direction:"IN")
20     address_sender: Address @relation(name: "Sender",
         direction:"IN")
21     address_reply_to: Address @relation(name: "ReplyTo",
         direction:"IN")
22   }
23
24   type Destination {
25     id: ID!
```

```
26      destination_role: String!
27      received_date: String!
28      message: Message! @relation(name: "Destination",
        direction:"IN")
29      address_to: [Address]! @relation(name: "To",
        direction:"IN")
30      address_cc: [Address] @relation(name: "Cc",
        direction:"IN")
31      address_bcc: [Address] @relation(name: "Bcc",
        direction:"IN")
32   }
33
34   type Message {
35      id: ID!
36      subject: String
37      comments: String
38      originator: Originator! @relation(name: "Originator",
        direction:"IN")
39      destinations: [Destination]! @relation(name:
        "HasDestination")
40      referencing: [Message] @relation(name: "Referencing")
41      in_reply_to: [Message] @relation(name: "InReplyTo")
42      keywords: [Keyword] @relation(name: "Tags")
43   }
44
45   type Keyword {
46      id: ID!
47      keyword: String!
48      messages: [Message] @relation(name: "Tags",
        direction:"IN")
49   }
50   ');
```

Note that I have added directions to the @relations, since Neo4j needs to know the semantics.

In the Neo4j desktop workbench the result is the display of an internal-use only metadata document, which describes the GraphQL schema.

The Neo4j-GraphQL plugin contains some useful procedures for working with GraphQL in Neo4j. One of the important ones is about visualizing the GraphQL schema as a graph data model, as shown in Figure 12-2.

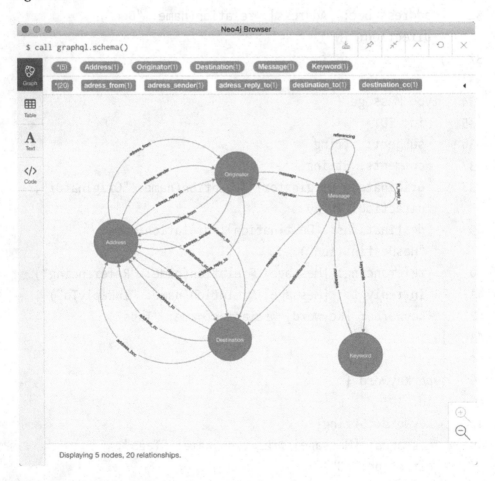

Figure 12-2. *Visualizing the GraphQL schema as a graph data model*

This lets you review the structure of the physical graph model. Corrections can be made on the GraphQL level, and the schema can be reprocessed.

Finally, by opening the GraphiQL GraphQL browser, we can see the GraphQL schema documentation. So, by now we are ready to query and mutate the data in the Neo4j graph database via the GraphQL API, as shown in Figure 12-3.

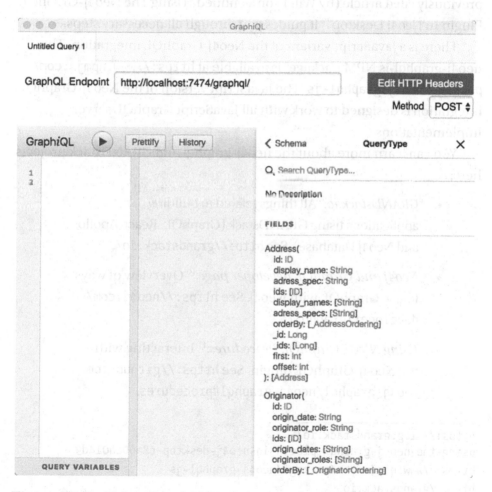

Figure 12-3. *Using GraphiQL to query and manipulate the graph data in Neo4j*

Using a Neo4j graph database as the underlying data store gives you a head start on your GraphQL project. Write your schema, tell it to Neo4j, and you are ready to enter data and query it by way of GraphQL.

Neo4j-GraphQL Resources

A good place to start getting involved with GraphQL and Neo4j is this previously cited article (by Will Lyon), entitled "Using The Neo4j-GraphQL Plugin In Neo4j Desktop".[7] It guides you through all necessary steps.

There is a JavaScript variant of the Neo4j-GraphQL integration. The neo4j-graphql-js NPM package[8] is available at `https://www.npmjs.com/package/neo4j-graphql-js`. The JavaScript version of the Neo4j-GraphQL integration is designed to work with all JavaScript GraphQL server implementations.

You can learn more about the neo4j-graphql and GRANDstack projects here:

- *GRANDstack.io*:[9] All things related to building applications using GRANDstack (GraphQL, React, Apollo, and Neo4j Database). See `http://grandstack.io/`.

- *Neo4j and GraphQL developer page*:[10] Overview of ways to use GraphQL with Neo4j. See `https://neo4j.com/developer/graphql/`.

- *Using Neo4j-GraphQL Procedures*:[11] Interacting with the Neo4j-GraphQL plugin. See `https://github.com/neo4j-graphql/neo4j-graphql#procedures`.

---

[7]`https://blog.grandstack.io/`
 `using-the-neo4j-graphql-plugin-in-neo4j-desktop-c8a60aa014d9`
[8]`https://www.npmjs.com/package/neo4j-graphql-js`
[9]`http://grandstack.io`
[10]`https://neo4j.com/developer/graphql/`
[11]`https://github.com/neo4j-graphql/neo4j-graphql#procedures`

- *Neo4j-GraphQL GitHub organization:*[12] Find the code and docs for Neo4j-GraphQL integrations here. See `https://github.com/neo4j-graphql`.

- *neo4j-graphql-cli:*[13] A command-line tool for quickly spinning up a GraphQL API using Neo4j-GraphQL on Neo4j Sandbox. See `https://www.npmjs.com/package/neo4j-graphql-cli`.

- *The Neo4j Slack Channel:*[14] A command-line tool for quickly spinning up a GraphQL API using Neo4j-GraphQL on Neo4j Sandbox. See `https://www.neo4j.com/slack`.

---

[12]`https://github.com/neo4j-graphql`
[13]`https://www.npmjs.com/package/neo4j-graphql-cli`
[14]`https://www.neo4j.com/slack`

AFTERWORD

Summary

Delivering high-quality APIs with good business value is perfectly possible and repeatable, provided you keep these 10 pieces of advice in mind:

- Design for the business—stay within its scope and definitions

- Understand the business concepts and their properties

- Name all relationships

- Understand all relationships and design the schema accordingly

- Pay special attention to cardinalities

- Get identities and uniqueness right

- Realize that design is a series of decisions, so you need to talk with the stakeholders

- Be very careful with many-to-many relationships

- Consider using data profiling or similar machine assistance in understanding the data

- Draw those concept and property graph diagrams!

The GraphQL approach has many benefits that seasoned data professionals will admire. It has a good potential of being a long-lasting thing; self-describing, structured result sets are good for everybody. The

© Thomas Frisendal 2018
T. Frisendal, *Visual Design of GraphQL Data*,
https://doi.org/10.1007/978-1-4842-3904-9

legacy technologies for interfacing with data were as good as they could be at the time they came about, but that is not good enough today. GraphQL is still young, but maturing, and everyone can benefit from having graph visualizations in there. The same goes for a visual, interactive version of GraphIQL, for end-users!

Oh, and remember: *Information is based on trust, and if business people do not trust or understand the data presented to them, they will stop using it!*

Be prepared to do the additional work, if necessary, based on circumstances. Make sure that what you deliver is visual and pretty. Then you are good to go.

This book is an ongoing project. Feedback is appreciated. Send an email to the author[1] at info@graphdatamodeling.com.

---

[1]`mailto:info@graphdatamodeling.com`

Index

A, B

Business flow
    API designers, 35
    business-level keys, 35
    database designs, 36
    key fields, 37
    network of objects and events, 35
    state changes, 37
    versions, 38
Business meaning
    API matter, 27
    applications/microservices, 27
    data names, 27
    establishing identity and
        uniqueness, 31
    finding standard data
        structures, 30

C

Company Location property, 31
Content matters
    custom schema directives, 41
    date and time, 40
    design, 43
    housekeeping, 39
    scalar data types, 40
Cypher, 81

D

Data model structure
    Customer-places-Order, 46
    generalization *vs.*
        specialization, 50
    inter-object relationships, 57
    linking phrase, 56
    many-to-many relationship,
        52, 54, 57
    objects/events, 60
    one-to-one relationships, 54
    originator, 55
    patchwork, 46
    properties, 55
    property graph, 51–52, 57
    property of relationship, 53
    self-references, 56
    supplier parts, 59
    ternary relationship, 52–53
    tools, 45
    type of relationship, 48
    use of properties, 54

E, F

Email
    data graph, 19
    Graphcool, 26

© Thomas Frisendal 2018
T. Frisendal, *Visual Design of GraphQL Data*,
https://doi.org/10.1007/978-1-4842-3904-9

Printed in the United States
By Bookmasters